To,

Dear Calum,

Best wishes to one of my best friends

Kind Regards

Data...the DNA of Business Intelligence

Ashok G. Vadgama
Motorola

Wayne McCleve
Motorola

Editor
Ron Bleeker
CAM-I

Consortium for Advanced
Manufacturing - International

6737 Brentwood Stair Road, Suite 214
Ft. Worth, TX 76112

ISBN: 1-59453-335-0

Bookman LLC
Publishing & Marketing
Providing Quality, Professional Author Services

www.BookmanMarketing.com

DEDICATION

This book is dedicated to my wife, Anita Vadgama, my children Kavita Vadgama and Rajeev Vadgama.

I would also like to dedicate this book to my mother, Mrs. Jaya Vadgama; my father, the late Mr. Gordhan Vadgama; my mother-in-law, Mrs. Anand Chhabra; and my father-in-law, the late Mr. Harbhajan Singh Chhabra.

Ashok G. Vadgama

Many have played a role in my data journey. I wish to recognize all those who have participated in the Motorola Sector Data and Configuration Management organization, those on my data quality team and specifically my mentor, Don Carlson, now the Senior Vice President of Information Quality for Bank of America. Their professionalism, understanding and dedication as we have made the data journey has proved to be some of the most rewarding years of my career thus far. My wife, Camette and daughters Brittney, Michelle, Jalee, Heidi, Kenna and Kinsey – you are my life and my joy; and lastly, I dedicate this book to my father Larry McCleve who passed away while it was being written. Dad, you are and have always been my hero.

Wayne McCleve

PROFESSIONAL ACKNOWLEDGEMENTS

This book would not have been possible if I had not worked with Mr. Don Carlson, now a Senior Vice-President for Information Quality at Bank of America.

I have had the pleasure of speaking at national and international industry conferences in the areas of strategic cost management, Activity Based Management (ABM), capacity planning, and value of data and processes. I was fortunate to have shared the podium with Dr. Bala Balachandran - Distinguished Professor of Accounting and Information Systems and Decision Sciences at J. L. Kellogg Graduate School of Management; Mohan Nair, Senior Marketing Executive Vice-President for Regence Group; and John Miller, author of the book "Implementing Activity Based Management in Daily Operations". I thank them for their contribution to my knowledge base.

I also wish to thank Mr. Ron Bleeker, Program Director of Cost Management Systems at CAM-I who underwrote and supported our efforts.

Ashok G. Vadgama

CONTRIBUTIONS

The authors would like to sincerely thank the following people for their kind contributions to the book:

Jeff Acklen – Motorola
Don Carlson – Bank of America
Julie Grimme – Motorola
Robert Holder – Motorola
Lynn Jankovsky – Motorola
Eric Limbert – Motorola
Betsy Roberts – Motorola
Dr. Walt Trybula – SEMATECH

We also thank the following people for their advance manuscript readings and feedback:

Don Carlson – Bank of America
Pat Dowdle – Process Advantage
Fritz Fielding – Motorola.
Terry Kroenung – Motorola

PREFACE

It was late Spring of 2002 when Ashok Vadgama first engaged CAM-I with the idea of studying and documenting the impact of data integrity on operational and financial performance.

I had always been intrigued and puzzled that managers are quick to concur with the notion that bad data impacts cost and thereby the proverbial "bottom line", but few if any were doing anything to rectify that impact. That complacency yields up responses such as "that's just the way it is", and finger pointing that "it's a systems problem!" Worse yet, some believe throwing money at the IT Department alone will fix it. It was encouraging that Motorola was taking pioneering strides to understand the problem and attempt to constructively improve performance by insuring that data foundational to decision support was both timely and accurate.

Ashok proposed that CAM-I underwrite capturing their findings and methodologies in a book. It was clear to me at the onset that this was a worthy and compelling undertaking and a meeting was arranged between us and his proposed co-author, Wayne McCleve. When we met some weeks later in Dallas and spent a day drafting an outline of the project, I came away with an even stronger conviction that this deliverable would indeed be valuable albeit long overdue.

With that agreed upon outline the project was inaugurated and writing DATA: The DNA of Business Intelligence was begun. During the ensuing journey of numerous interim author meetings, progress and success stories were shared at various CAM-I sponsored assemblies and conferences. With each event came a flurry of confirmations from attendees thirsty for more information and "how to" in this arena.

On the other hand, I certainly don't mean to imply that this mission was easy and didn't have the attendant challenges that come with every publishing project. On the contrary. A quick review of the number of contributors to the content herein and an understanding of the difficulties associated with the collaborative process required to incorporate those contributions confirms that compiling and organizing this information has been monumental.

Beyond that, their work is inarguably landmark in an arena for which they will be credited with coining the term "Data Integrity." To that end it has truly been a pleasure to serve as Editor on the book and to shepherd it through the final galley proofs and into print.

My thanks to my wife Karen for her constant encouragement, patience and forgiving nature with the long hours that are always a part of bringing a book to fruition. My sincerest congratulations to both Ashok and Wayne for their vision and tenacity in ushering in a

milestone work that is sure to be followed by many authors to come.

Ron Bleeker
CMS Program Director, CAM-I

TABLE OF CONTENTS

Data… the DNA of Business Intelligence

FIGURES & TABLES

Chapter 8

Chapter 9

Chapter 10

Chapter 11

1 CHAPTER

DATA FUELS THE ENTERPRISE

INTRODUCTION

Data plays a key role in driving decisions; it fuels information that is used by decision makers to create competitive advantage. Data is representation of facts. By putting it in context to give it meaning, data becomes the raw material from which information is produced. Most Information Technology project failures are due to bad data. A survey of key industries shows that bad data is the most significant problem with many Information Technology departments. With recent strides in E-Enterprise it is even more important to ensure that the data is good. Customers and suppliers require accurate data to know when and in what quantity to buy and to deliver.

1.1 DATA & INFORMATION

Larry English[1] in his book "Improving Data Warehouse

---

[1] Larry P. English Improving Data Warehouse and Business Information Quality, John Wiley & Sons

and Business Information Quality" has described the value of information as:

Information = Data + Definition + Presentation

Knowledge = People + Information + Significance

Wisdom = People + Knowledge + Action

Larry English's research also showed that the cost of bad data can be 10% to 20% percent of revenue. 20% to 40% percent of an organization's IT budget may be spent on addressing data issues instead of doing valueadded development.

1.1.1 Critical Need for Enterprise Data

Critical needs reside in the areas of…

Financials
Statutes, regulations, GAAP, disclosures
Enterprise Systems, CRM, Modeling and Simulation scenarios
Factory execution systems
The E-Everything World
Customer Quality
Requirements for data extraction, data mining and reporting
Capacity planning, cost-of-ownership models

Difficulty in accessing critical data compromises the effectiveness and results in downtime and workflow inefficiencies.

Finance becomes an owner of paper-based instructions scattered on multiple pieces of paper on out-of-date spreadsheets in multiple locations.

People do not trust the data quality so they create their own data and processes, which results in disparate databases and standards, the need for qualitative processes, multiple systems of record, and increases in the level of spending for implementing enterprise systems.

We have so many problems with data and at what cost?

1.1.2 Benchmark Data

In oil and gas industries, per many oil and gas publications, 35% of data is incorrect, incomplete, misfiled, inaccurate, or does not exist. A large processing plant can waste up to $3M per year due to poor data quality.

The semiconductor industry is highly capital intensive, similar to the oil and gas industries. About 80% of the cost is attributable to fixed assets. The cost of maintenance is also very high. A significant part of the performance metrics is equipment utilization in terms of down time, set up time, waiting time, and from the perspective of Cost of Ownership. The Cost of Ownership is pre-negotiated with equipment suppliers. Therefore, bad data has huge impact in terms of top line growth and cost to such industries.

1.1.3 Data Value Chain Elements

At the end of the data value chain, customers are benefited by a high level of customer service, directly attributed to having access to data and information.

At the beginning of the data value chain, suppliers need to know what to buy, where they want it to be sent, when they want to get it and what they are willing to pay for it.

Answers to all these questions and the consequences are:

- Hard to access data – extra work for your employees
- Lack of data – factory down time
- Bad data – lots of exchange of what is given vs. what is needed.

Your customer needs to know what you make, what your product/service is, how they buy it, what their order status is.

These result in:

- Hard to access data – lose customer
- Lack of data – frustration resulting in a loss of the customer
- Bad data – extreme frustration on the customer's part

Poor quality data is most often the output of disconnects in the related data or business processes. Cost of bad data can be measured in terms of trustworthiness, timeliness and improvement required. The cost is measured in terms of extra input, extra storage, and extra meetings to fix problems, multiple systems of records and impact of errors.

Data is scattered all around and lack of a single repository for a given data element has a big impact on cost. Collapsing multiple systems of records to a single system of record can realize a 50% saving for an enterprise as the authors have experienced.

There exists a supply chain tolerance of data in the enterprise. As data propagates its way through systems, or is derived from various data elements into a resulting data element, the "goodness" of the data becomes a product of each stage or data source in the process flow. This can be illustrated by the analogous supply chain tolerance in a typical semiconductor operation per the following chart:

At each stage of manufacturing there is an associated yield of good die on the wafer. The resulting total yield of die on the wafer is a simple mathematical product of the yield of each stage ($Y_1 \times Y_2 \times Y_3 \times \ldots Y_n = Y_{total}$). A seemingly high yield, or conversely small failure percentage, at each stage adds up to significant impact on over all yield. A twenty-stage semiconductor process each with a 99% yield would result in an 81% total yield. A typical semiconductor process has over 200 stages. With the same stage yield values this would result in 13% total yield! The same law holds true for data. The percentage of good data at the point of use is derived in the same way. There may be fewer stages in a typical data flow but the usual percentage of bad data is much higher than in the semiconductor example with 5% to 10% being typical.

Figure 1.1: Supply Chain Tolerance Analysis.

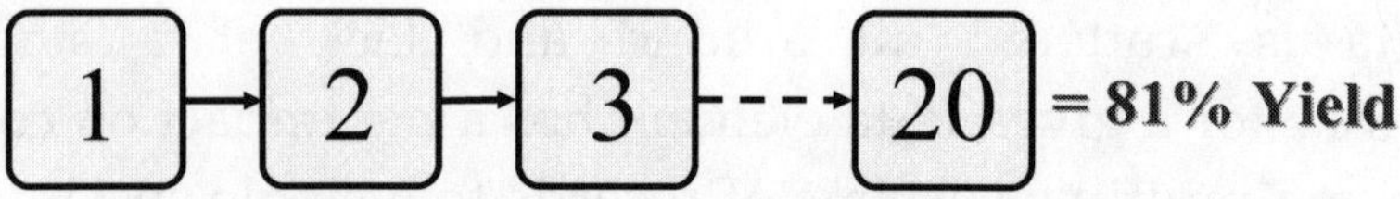

(20 manufacturing steps at 99% Yield each)

- **Chips ~200 steps. 99% Yield at Each Step will Result in Final Yield = 13% Yield**
- ***The Same Relationship is True with Data!***
- **Error Rates are Higher (5-10% is common)**

1.1.4 Total Data Value Chain

Figure 1.1 illustrates the data connections and paths in a single company through three major stages of fabrication for the bill of materials data set. Every node and line has an associated percentage of good/bad data. By using tracking methods and doing trend analysis, a company can intensify correcting the upstream sources of bad data and also prioritize the problems within the data value chain. Other metrics and tools can be put in place to provide enterprise wide visibility of the data health and costs.

Figure 1.2: The Data Chain = Fab (Supply Chain)

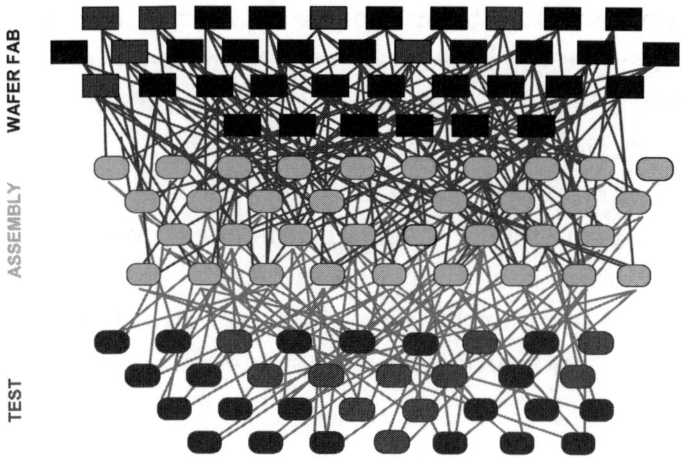

1.2 Bill of Material

Here is how one might look at a Bill of Material (BOM) in your company:

Table 1.3: Sample Bill of Material

Data Element	% of Cost	# of Errors Fixed	Errors as % of Cost
Elements of BOM	3%	37080	2%
Packaging	10%	8225	36%
Cycle Time, Yield	85%	462430	22%
Routing	2%	2133	40%

The numbers above are a good representation in many companies. The number of errors has a non-linear relationship to total cost as at every stage of the process the cost increases exponential.

If a company has to spend money correcting bad data, why not manage data? Data is used to manage information. Information fuels the enterprise. The amount of time spent looking for critical data is unacceptable. The E-revolution will force companies to get data and processes right, or drive them out of business. Cost of mistakes equates to lost production, and customer dissatisfaction leads to a non critical role in the market place. Can you afford not to focus on good data and processes – a strategic asset (DNA) for your company?

1.3 Return on Investment (ROI)

Now let us look at the return on investment for the enterprise.

Return on Investment (ROI) for collapsing multiple systems of record (The system, including the original data, application code, and data repository, that controls the update and maintenance of a specific set of data) have a direct impact on cycle time and yield. Saving cycle time based on down stream multiple systems, instead of one system of record results in capital utilization improvements and people productivity gains.

People productivity can be measured in terms of ease of access to data, better usage of time, reduced inventory to manage, ease of scheduling and planning due to goodness of data, and impact on on-time delivery.

A single place to access people data, like contacts, will result in a saving of up to $5M dollars assuming the company has 4,000 employees.

The ROI on implementation of enterprise systems based on good data is huge. The common reason why such implementations fail is bad data – garbage in, garbage out. Once bad data is fed into a new system, it becomes a mammoth task to clean it due to the interdependencies of other modules within the enterprise systems.

The cost saving of implementation can be realized up front by working on the enterprise data first resulting into savings and ROI.

1.4 Trustworthy, Timely, Seamless Data

Data does fuel the enterprise but it must be trustworthy, timely and seamless.

How does one recognize it when one sees it?

14.1 Trustworthy

- Data has a known and widely accepted relationship to actual values
- Data sources are acknowledged subject matter experts
- Data and metadata is created, maintained and measured in accordance with a documented authoritative process
- Data is validated/updated on a regular basis using well defined rules and metrics of data quality

- There is only one system of record
- Data is not, and cannot be entered or changed in any data system other than the system of record
- Data and changes to the data are tightly controlled (appropriate level of Configuration Management)
- Data level of detail is sufficient to ensure accurate results from all using systems/processes/tools
- Invalid (per defined business rules) data cannot be entered (tool enabled data entry validation) and data in the data stores is routinely checked for corruption
- Metadata is periodically checked for indications of data being "co-opted" and used for purposes inconsistent with the data element definition

1.4.2 Timely

- Data is available when needed and where needed
    - New data (types and elements) are introduced as needed to support changes in the business
    - The data "portfolio" is managed based on the data life cycle required by the business
- Data is validated/updated based on the rate of change in the process/business the data represents and the frequency at which the data is used
- Data delivery to interdependent tools and processes is understood, documented, and synchronized to meet business need
- High (90+) percentile data cycle time (data input to final approval) is less than the time between

scheduled runs of the processes using the data (for all critical operational data)

1.4.3 Seamless

- There should be only one system of record for the data
- Data only needs to be entered once: then it is automatically distributed to those using processes
- Tools and processes which use the data, use the data from the system of record
- Other data needed to support essential business processes available with no "holes" (missing data)
- All data has a valid value (per the defined business rules)
- All data has a defined effective and expiration date and there are no "temporal" overlaps or disconnects in the data
- When data is needed that is an aggregate of the data in the system of record, the aggregate data is created from the detail data
- Time-phased data is revalidated just before the date the data is to become effective

1.5 Key Messages

- The Value is in the Use of "good" Data to Make Decisions
- Data and Information is the Second Most Valuable Asset to the Organization

- The Cost of Data to The Enterprise is Big
- The Cost of Bad Data to The Enterprise is Bigger
- There are pockets of success but there is much more to do!
- Clean the Data and drive processes to keep it clean!
- And follow active Configuration Management.

The importance of Information Quality and data is growing.

1.5.1 Key Message Support

Many companies are setting up Information Quality areas to focus on data and processes. There are more Information Quality seminars and meetings.

There are more job openings in this area. A lot of emphasis is given to data for enterprise resource planning. Business process methodologies are looked at from the perspective of ROI and in some areas application of activity based analysis.

CHAPTER RECAP

This chapter is foundational to understanding the importance of information quality. The cost of data, ROI's, and benchmark information should have prompted understanding of the magnitude of damage that can be done to an organization if bad data is tolerated. Data is pertinent all across the value chain and it is easier to correct problems at the beginning of the supply chain than to wait to address them once bad data has polluted other systems. Trustworthy, timely and seamless data should be on everyone's performance plan.

2 CHAPTER

DATA IS DNA

INTRODUCTION

We humans like to explain things in simplistic ways. One simplistic way is the use of a metaphor, a figure of speech that uses the comparison of two or more seemingly unrelated objects to give a greater conceptual understand of one of the objects. This is not laziness but rather efficiency, for a metaphor can convey much information in a few words,such as Shakespeare's "All the world's a stage," or "It's a dog's life," or "Life is like a box of chocolates," or "Time is money," and so on. The concept being conveyed in this book is that "Data is the DNA of Business".

There are not many rules to the use of metaphors, but one rule is essential: that is, that the characteristics of the objects be known to the reader. If one or both of the objects are not understood on their own, then the conceptual message is not delivered. Therefore, to be fully equipped to explore the book's title, we must understand what Data, DNA and Business are.

What is data? There are numerous definitions, each depending on the context in which Data is being used. In programming, data could be defined as stored values classified into several different types such as integer, real, text etc.; in science, as observations or measurements; in law enforcement, as the facts; and in business, as the elements which automated or manual systems are built around to produce a product, service or information for decision making.

Let's add another definition to the lexicon. ***Data is the smallest quantum element of information possible; it is the atom of information.*** Oops, we have slipped into metaphors again. Like an atom of lead, if split, you have something completely different, not two smaller chucks of lead. If data is broken into parts, it no longer has the same meaning. For instance, if part number KU42764b, a cell phone, is broken into KU42 and 764b, it is unlikely that these two strings of charters represent two other cell phones. This would truly be a strange part scheme. There is a caveat here, though. Companies are notorious about embedding information in part numbers, a bad data practice. KU42764b could be broken into KU, a location code, 42764 a unique part number, and "b" a first revision of 42764. Here KU42764b is really not a part number but a molecule of information composed of unique data atoms. 42762 is the part number. The molecule KU42764b is part information centered on a part identifier with relevant meta data regarding revision history and the location where it was assembled.

An everyday example that is illustrative of the difference between the information molecule and the data atom is

"ADDRESS". An address is commonly composed of the data atoms of STREET NUMBER, STREET, CITY, STATE and ZIPCODE. If you wished to create an online form to collect an address it would be a poor choice to create a field called "Address" in which all of the above elements would be inserted by the user. If you did, your unfortunate Information Technology support person would have to create a complex script to parse out the elements of address so that the data elements could be stored and used properly for a host of intended purposes for which you might want to use this data. Instead, as you have undoubtedly experienced, separate fields are created for the user of the online form to enter in each data element of address.

In the real world, data elements are combined to create molecules of information. These molecules are in turn combined to create other aggregations such as a bill of materials, a financial report, a schedule, etc. So this is the relationship of data to information and the meaning of data in our metaphor.

We need now to define DNA. As for the definition of business, we will make the leap of faith that the reader has a good handle on it.

If this were a book on genetics we would spend significant time defining DNA; but this isn't a book on genetics. What we want to accomplish is to define DNA in its prevailing common meaning, something like "DNA is the chemical code for making a living organism." Some attributes of DNA are also helpful in conveying our metaphor, such as "DNA can be broken but the resulting organism will likely be deformed, dysfunctional or unviable." Also, the majority of the code in DNA is commented out. That is to say it does nothing when the code is executed, so the small nuggets of code that are executed are important to understand as well as their relationship to other nuggets.

With data, DNA and business defined, the "Data is DNA" metaphor immediately conveys much about the integral nature of data to business. For instance, we can extrapolate the metaphor to cancer, which is often caused by defective DNA, and the resulting severe effect to the body. In business as with the body much in the way of resources may be targeted to fix or just maintain viability. The good news is that unlike cancer, we have the cure to the data pathogen. The difficulty in business usually resides in making a correct diagnosis.

With these concepts in our pocket we are ready for the illumination of the remaining chapters in the context of the metaphor "Data the DNA of business".

2.1 Data: Not "Sexy", But Critical For E-Business Success

The success of (e-business) is completely dependent on quality, completeness, and accessibility of data. This section discusses the issues behind this statement.

2.2 e-Business Definition

Within the context of this section, "e-Business" can be viewed as a collection of systems and the interactions that they support between customers and suppliers as shown in Figure 2.1.

Figure 2.1: e-Business Systems and Interactions

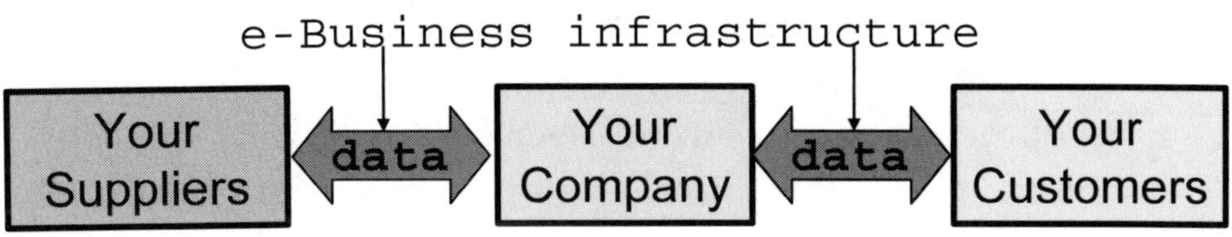

In Figure 2.1, assume that "Your Company" is a computer or system. The customers and suppliers could be:

a. People. In this case, the type of e-business is referred to as business-to-consumers (B2C).
b. Computers or systems. In this case, the type of e-business is referred to as business-to-business (B2B).

2.3 e-Business without Data

From a data perspective, e-business is all about providing data to customers and/or suppliers and getting data from customers and/or suppliers. As consumers, most people's initial exposure to e-business consists of people trying to get data from a company's web site. Imagine how successful the following B2C e-businesses would be:

a. amazon.com with no book titles or authors
b. ditech.com with no current mortgage rates
c. priceline.com with no flight schedules
d. google.com with no words to search

Book titles, mortgage rates, flight schedules, and words are all examples of data. It is safe to say that without data, none of these dot com businesses would still be in business. Therefore, one of the critical e-business challenges that must be overcome is getting data and making that data available to customers (and suppliers).

2.4 COMMON DATA PITFALLS

There are many data pitfalls found in e-business implementations. These pitfalls are explored below.

2.4.1 Data Collection Not Important

Many times, before data can be provided to a customer or a supplier, it must first be collected. Here, "collection" includes gathering data together from disparate sources, creating new data, and maintaining existing data which can change over time. Data collection can be tedious and time-consuming. It is, therefore, often assigned to lower-level employees. Because of this, data collection is often assumed to be unimportant. Resources, especially high-performance employees, are assigned to other responsibilities such as data presentation. This will be discussed later.

If data presentation functionality is created, it is assumed that the data will be collected by somebody in order to use the data presentation functionality. To paraphrase the catch phrase in Field of Dreams[2], it is sometimes assumed that "if we build the data presentation functionality, the data will come".

Another reason that data collection is assumed to be not important is that data presentation functionality is often developed by people who are not data owners. Because developers are not data owners, they often have little knowledge of the work that is required to collect data. Lack of knowledge is a breeding ground for assumptions. Often, the assumption is "my work is more important than all other work".

For decades, "Usenet" news groups have existed as organized forums for communication about specific subjects. News groups, in fact, pre-date the internet. Nobody thought to archive news group postings in a systemic fashion.

Realizing that news groups contain a great deal of useful data (and information), Google invested a great deal of resources and time to track down every possible source of archived news group messages (also called "postings"). Google combined the old news group postings (some going back to 1981) with current news group postings. As a result, Google now offers its customers access to more than 700 million news group postings...and counting.[3]

---

[2] Robinson, Phil Alden, dir. Field of Dreams. Perf. Kevin Kostner, Amy Madigan, and James Earl Jones. Universal, 1989.

[3] See http://groups.google.com/

2.4.2 One-time Event

Companies can come to an unexpected realization that data is needed, but is not currently available. Fixing this problem can be treated as a one-time event, otherwise known as a "fire drill". All available personnel are told to drop what they are doing and to concentrate on the new need.

Fire drills can get a lot of results in a short period of time. Unfortunately, fire drills have many negatives including:

a. Activities that personnel involved in the fire drill were working on get delayed. This may have negative consequences for other projects.
b. Actions that are taken are often not fully planned. Sometimes, the actions that get taken are not even completely thought out. The quality of work suffers because shortcuts are taken.
c. Involved personnel typically do what is most efficient for them, so they can get back to their real work. This may adversely affect other fire drill personnel's activities.
d. Generally, there are no common processes. Because of this, necessary steps are often skipped or duplicated by others. This is another example of wasted resources.
e. Little or no consideration may be given to the future. Will data quality (if any) stay high? If there is a future need for the same type(s) of data, will people remember what they did during this fire drill?

Fire drill negatives usually outweigh positives. In most cases, fire drills should be avoided.

2.4.3 Data Optionalism

Some companies centralize the creation of business processes and require all organizations to adhere to these processes. Some companies do not attempt to create business processes centrally. Instead, each organization is encouraged to create business processes that meet its needs without any consideration being given to the affect those processes will have on the company.

In other companies, processes are created centrally, but organizations are allowed to choose whether or not they will adopt those processes, which are usually called "guidelines". Since process adoption is optional, this practice is referred to as "optionalism". Optionalism can apply to business processes that deal with the creation and maintenance of data.

Data process optionalism produces confusing results for customers:

a. Different data definitions. For example, "voltage" may be defined by one organization as being the maximum voltage, while another organization might consider "voltage" to be a typical voltage.
b. Different data collection frequencies. If one organization collects data when the data is created or changes, while another organization collects data

every month or every fiscal quarter, the currency of the data will depend on the organization that provides the data. Unless customers only deal with one organization, the customers may get confused.

c. Different data collection methods. Manually entered data can contain typographical errors. Copy-and-paste from a document means that data is not updated until the document is completely revised. Data that is collected on spreadsheets may be e-mailed to others for review thereby creating delays.

2.5 ACHIEVING LOWEST COST DATA

Collecting and maintaining data does not have to be expensive. Three ways to keep costs down are discussed and an emerging trend is described.

2.5.1 Plan, Plan, Plan

When they realize that something needs to be done, many organizations practice "Ready, shoot, aim!". In other words, they do things before they really understand what needs to be done.

An old cliché says, "An ounce of prevention is worth a pound of cure". This can be restated for the business world as, "A week of planning is worth months of doing it right the second time"[4]. If one avoids doing things over again, then one avoids the cost of doing things over again.

---

[4] Eric Limbert. AICPA/CAM-I Cost and Performance Management Symposium. May 22, 2003.

Note that an emphasis on planning is actually one of the cornerstones of good project management. Careful planning can result in high quality data being available for use by e-business when needed.

2.5.2 Use Standards

Leveraging the work of others is an easy way to keep costs low. There are many industry standards which could be reused by organizations which create data standards. Some of these standards are focused on the needs of e-business, including the communication of data.

Industry standards can facilitate e-business by providing a common understanding of:

a. Units of measure
b. Data formats
c. Message structure

Many standards organizations exist. Among these are W3C[5], RosettaNet[6], ANSI[7], EIA[8], and UCC[9]. Some of these are focused on specific industries or user communities. While that does not necessarily mean that the standards could not be used outside of their intended audiences, caution should be taken before completely adopting them outside of intended uses.

---

[5] World Wide Web Consortium. http://www.w3c.org/
[6] RosettaNet. http://www.rosettanet.org/
[7] American National Standards Institute. http://www.ansi.org/
[8] Electronic Industries Alliance. http://www.eia.org/
[9] Uniform Code Council. http://www.uc-council.org/

2.5.3 Measure, Measure, Measure

Earlier in this section, mention was made of the necessity to "plan, plan, plan!" A plan includes the following elements:

a. Baseline understanding of where the project is starting from. This is sometimes referred to as the "as is" situation.
b. What the expected project results, or goal, will be. This is sometimes referred to as the "to be" situation.
c. How to get from "as is" to "to be".

To ensure that an e-business data project's goal is met, progress must be measured against the goal. As the old adage says, "You get what you measure". Because the project is data related, implementing metrics (i.e., measurements of progress) should be easy to do. When the project is completed, it might be beneficial to continue using the project's metrics to ensure that success is sustained over time.

Metrics can be text-based, spreadsheets, or graphical examples of which are shown in Figure 2.2.

Figure 2.2: Metric Examples

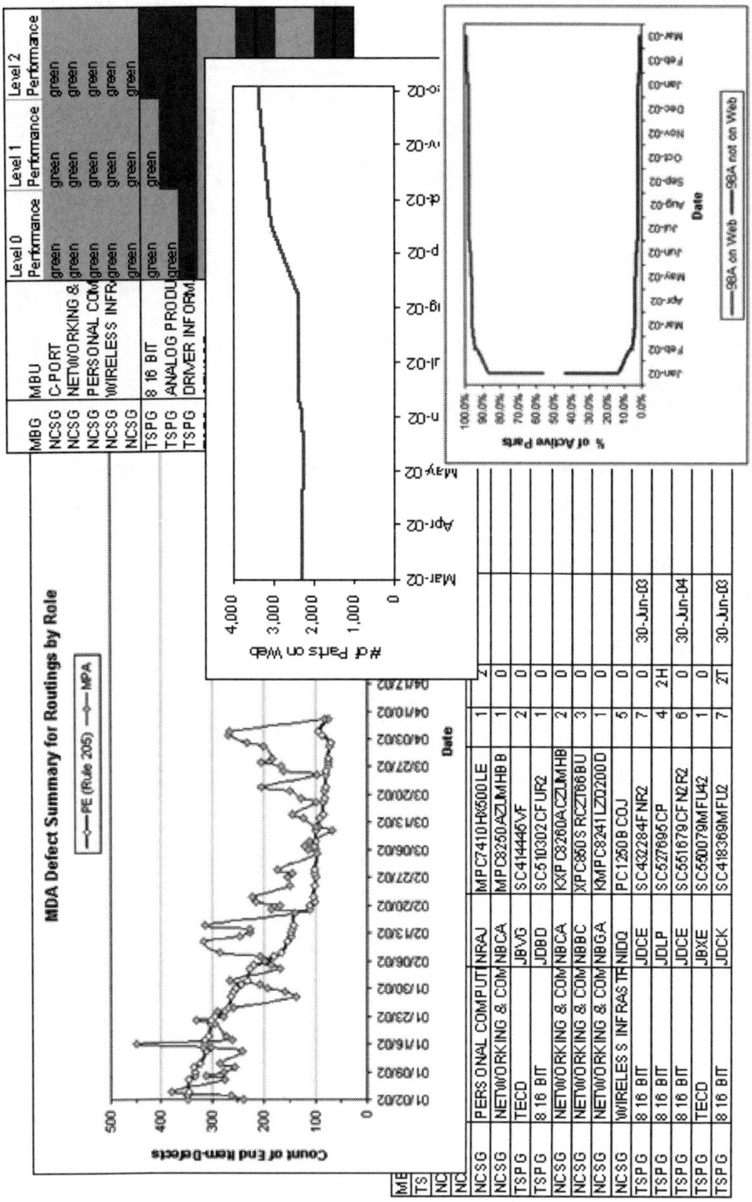

To keep costs low, do not measure for the sake of measurement. Instead, measure what is important. In other words, measure issues that will most directly impact project success.

It should be mentioned that measurement is an element of control, one of the project management phases.

2.6 INFOMEDIARIES

Realizing that they do not have a core competency in data collection, maintenance, and presentation,
some companies have chosen to subcontract these tasks. These companies can organize data to be presented to e-business partners or can aggregate the e-business data of others (usually suppliers) so that the client company can access the data with a single "look and feel" (called "normalization"). Data aggregators are sometimes called "infomediaries".

Infomediaries can extract (mine) data from client documents. The biggest positive of this is that the client company does not need to change their existing processes. Also, if infomediaries enable their clients to retain their existing processes, the clients do not reduce their costs by using infomediaries. Actually, the opposite occurs since the client company must both support their existing processes and pay the infomediary, a recurring cost.

2.7 DATA CURRENCY

Customers and suppliers need e-business data to be current. The word "current" is subjective. Data does not have to be real-time in order to be current. There is no reason to communicate new or changed data immediately if the users (customers, suppliers, or your company) do not want to receive it or use it immediately. Real-time data communication typically costs more than daily, weekly, monthly, or quarterly data communication.

2.8 GOOD PROJECT MANAGEMENT

In this chapter, the need for planning and control has been mentioned. These are two phases of project management. e-Business data will also benefit from adherence to effective use of other project management phases including:

a. Definition. Complete definition of an e-business data project provides benefits including clear project scope and identified executive sponsor.
b. Execution.
c. Closure. Capturing lessons learned will help ensure that future e-business data projects are implemented successfully.

For more information about project management, it is recommended that the reader contact the Project Management Institute.[10]

2.9 DATA DELIVERY & PRESENTATION

Having e-business data without a way to deliver and present the data to/from customers or suppliers is pointless. Many different delivery and presentation methods exist. See Figure 2.3 for an example of this. The oldest method is to put the data in printed documents (e.g., product catalogs, data sheets).

Figure 2.3: Delivery & Presentation Methods

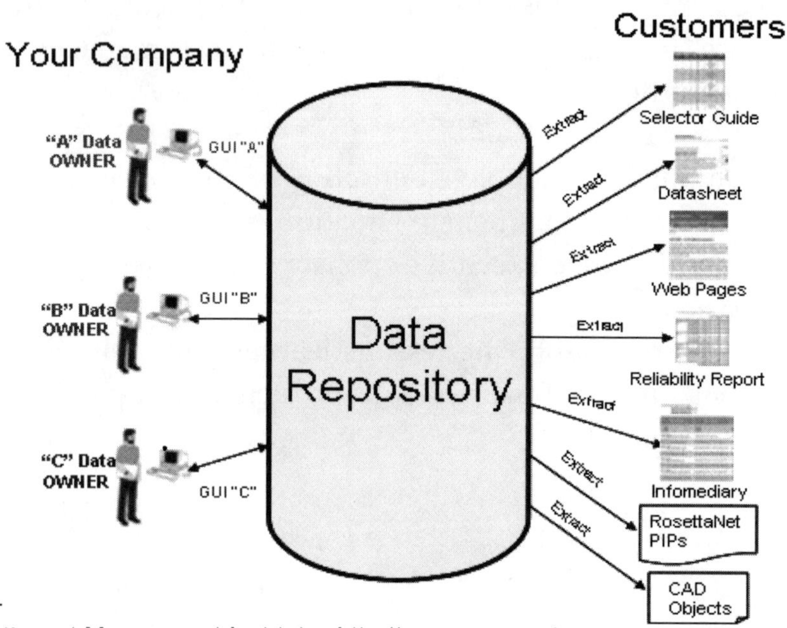

[10] Project Management Institute. http://www.pmi.org/

Other data delivery and presentation methods include FTP (file transfer protocol), HTTP (hypertext transfer protocol, the web), EDI (electronic data interchange), etc. Many of these formats support continued use of documents to communicate data, although the documents must be electronic (e.g., Adobe PDF, Microsoft Excel).

Selection of the most appropriate method(s) of e-business data delivery and presentation can be tricky. One must consider the following:

a. Technical maturity of both the sender and the receiver of the e-business data. Selection of a delivery and/or presentation method that is beyond the technical maturity of either party does not make sense unless the work required to implement and sustain the delivery method will be subcontracted to a company experienced in the delivery method.
b. Cost. The cost of e-business data delivery implementation and maintenance must be justifiable based on factors such as productivity improvement, customer satisfaction, or increased sales/purchase levels.
c. Extensibility. A delivery method that is implemented for one customer or partner may need to be extended to either include additional data or additional customers or suppliers.

2.10 EXAMPLES OF POOR E-BUSINESS DATA USE

There are many examples of poor e-business use of data. For example, it used to be that searches for the word "phone" on the Motorola web site[11] resulted in dozens of pages describing semiconductors. Although the pages all contained the word "phone", users who were actually looking for information about Motorola phones were probably disappointed, or worse.

Virtually every travel provider -- airlines, buses, and trains -- has a web site where users can enter their departure city and their arrival city. As long as the travel provider supports travel between both cities, the web site will then provide information about the trips. This is not the case for Amtrak's[12] web site. There, users must know the layout of Amtrak's tracks. If not traveling in a straight line, users must manually set up each straight-line leg of their trip themselves. The data exists in Amtrak's web site, but Amtrak has not chosen to make its use simple, as have Amtrak's competitors and peers in other countries.

Shopping at Sam's Club requires the payment of annual membership fees. Recently, a Sam's Club member was going through the check-out line only to be informed that his membership was about to expire. The option was provided to pay for a membership renewal with their other purchases – very efficient use of e-business data. This option was accepted and membership was immediately renewed. Two

---

[11] Motorola. http://www.motorola.com/

[12] Amtrak is a passenger train travel service provider located in the United States. http://www.amtrak.com/

weeks later, a notice was received in the mail saying that membership was about to expire. In small print, the notice said that the mailing was based on information (data) from a month before.

Capital One[13] spends a great deal of money on television and direct mail advertisements for its credit cards in the United States. Getting a Capital One credit card does not result in the cessation of direct mail ads. After receiving six or seven direct mail ads more than a month after getting a Capital One credit card, one might be tempted to ask, "Don't they know that I already have one in my wallet?".

Many other examples of poor e-business data use exist. Many result in customer frustration, anger, or refusal to do future business. Others result in unnecessary cost for the company. Some result in both.

2.11 CORRECT E-BUSINESS DATA USE

While there are many examples of bad e-business data use, there are also many example of good e-business data use. These have one characteristic in common: The people who designed these good e-business data uses put themselves in their intended customer's shoes. The audience's needs and wants were considered first, before the needs and wants of the company or organization.

Questions were asked such as: What data do users want to get? How do they want to get the data? How often do they want to get the data? An example of putting the

---

[13] Capital One. http://www.capitalone.com/

customers needs and wants first can be found at Fairchild Semiconductor[14]. Fairchild Semiconductor's "Customer First" e-business initiative has the published goal of "...allowing our customers...to do business with Fairchild the way they want to conduct business."

CHAPTER RECAP

One should never underestimate the importance of data for e-business. With appropriate e-business data processes, uses, delivery, and presentation, customers and/or suppliers can be delighted. Without them, customers and/or suppliers can become confused, frustrated, or even angry.

---

[14] Fairchild Semiconductor. http://www.fairchildsemi.com/

3 CHAPTER

DATA RELATED TO INFORMATION TECHNOLOGY

INTRODUCTION

When looking at the process flow where data and information systems are concerned, it is important to examine all areas of the supply chain. Emphasis on customer retention and demand for information from suppliers and customers has further elevated the imperative of enterprise data integrity. This chapter examines the linkage of data and information and the impact of errors.

3.1 SUPPLY CHAIN DATA

As we stated in the previous chapters, data plays a key role in driving decisions; it fuels information which is used by decision makers to create competitive advantage. Data is a representation of facts.

Companies with Customer Relationship Management (CRM) focus are gaining competitive advantage. This is important as it has been stated by Dr. Bala V. Balachandran:[15] "Total customer satisfaction can drive the company to a bankruptcy". This is very common in the industrial sector as all the companies in a downturn time are pursuing the same customers. Competition becomes fierce and customer demand for price cuts, special promotions and relationships become the key overriding principle.

According to the research by IDC[16] organizations that have successfully implemented and utilized analytical CRM applications generated a median return of 55 percent on their investment. Needless to say that to carry out good analysis, you need good data sets.

3.2 ORDER FULFILLMENT PROCESS

Figure 3.1: Order Fulfillment Process

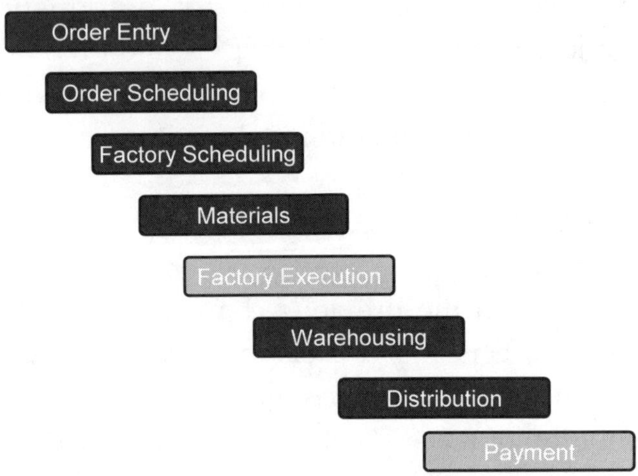

[15] Dr. Bala V. Balachandran, J. L. Kellogg Distinguished Professor of Accounting Information and Management.
[16] For more information about ICD, visit their web site at http://www.idc.com/.

The above chart on the order fulfillment process is a good representation of customer data flow required in a company. The first step is order entry. The authors have found in their experience that data quality problems start from data collection at the order entry level. This has an impact on the entire supply chain as far as scheduling and getting product out of the door is concerned. Factory scheduling ends up with an incorrect bill of material and routing. This will also impact material usage and factory execution systems.

3.3 SUPPLY CHAIN MANAGEMENT

The impact of bill of material on the distribution problems (due to incorrect routing) and finally the payment to supplier will result in a systemic problem that is very difficult and cumbersome to correct. Enterprise systems work on the notion of good data entry point. Due to the robustness of the system, the data is shared all around.

Figure 3.2 shows the same information shared in multiple modules of supply chain. A company with a good process framework is able to articulate the use of information throughout the supply chain. The whole notion of enterprise architecture is discussed in chapter 7.

As implementation is a modular approach, the first module where the data is impacted is the base module, where the entire foundation of core data and processes reside. Connectivity to manufacturing, distributors, retailers and customers is enabled by a sound work flow process.

Figure 3.2: Supply Chain Management Linked by Data & Information

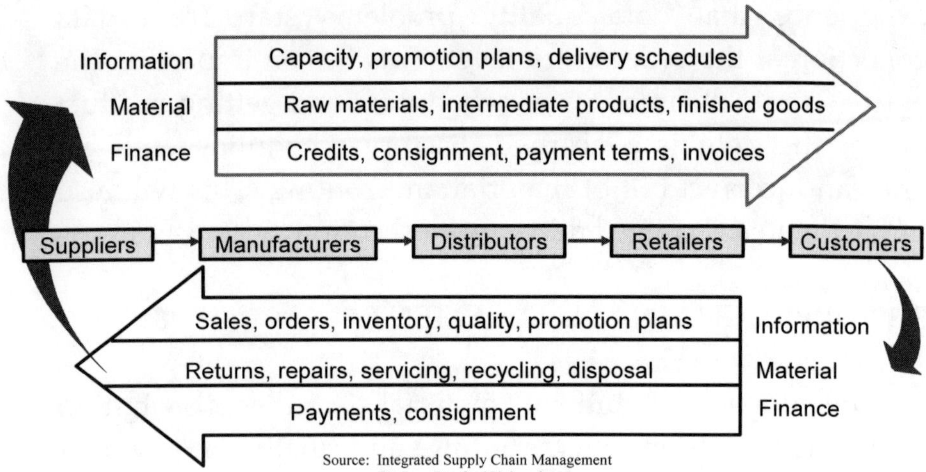

Source: Integrated Supply Chain Management
Dr. Lee, Stanford University

In Figure 3.2, raw material codes, product codes and finished goods codes play a significant role in the data flow from delivery schedules to consignment. It is important to do a data thread analysis (discussed in chapter 6) before implementing any connectivity to other systems like customer loyalty or CRM. This is what many companies do not understand, based on what the authors have experienced. Hence, bad planning of getting to customer satisfaction by good information will result in on-time delivery problems, wrong product shipped and incorrect locations and an inaccurate pricing model. Many companies have started using the data threads to compile target costing for their pricing models.

3.4 NEW PART PARAMETER PROCESS

Figure 3.3: New Part Parameter Process

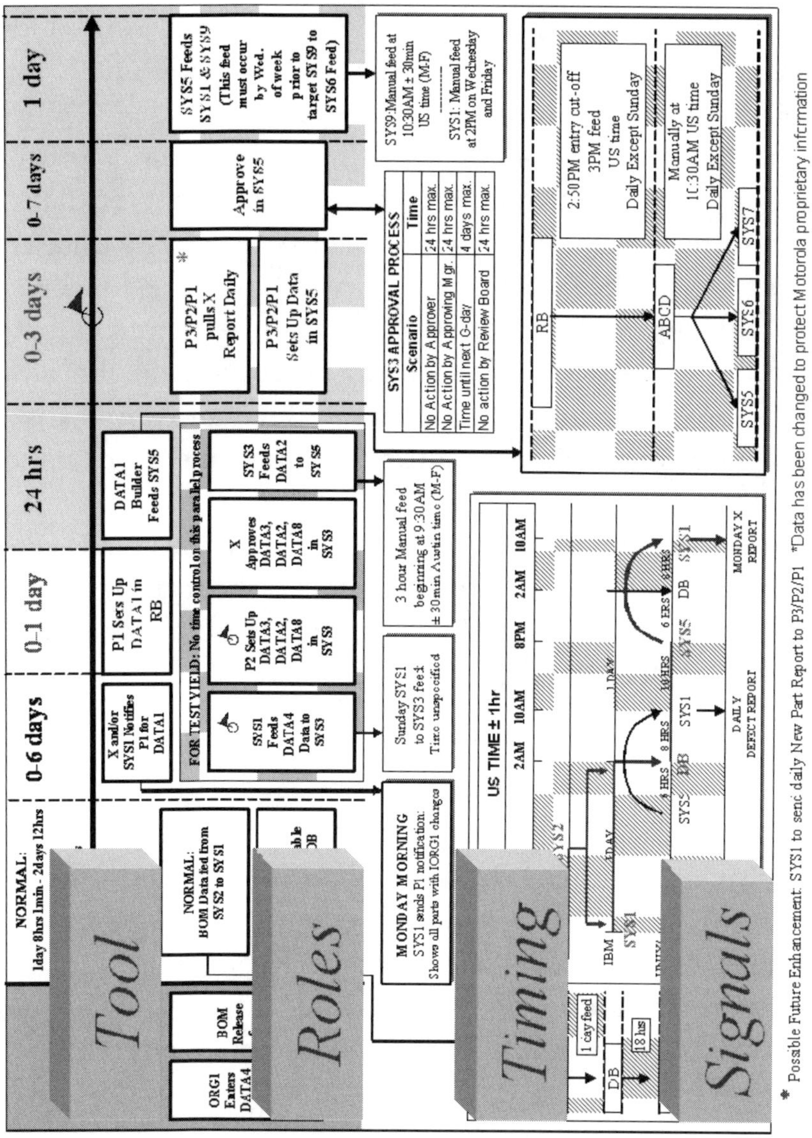

Scenario	Time
No Action by Approver	24 hrs max.
No Action by Approving Mgr.	24 hrs max.
Time until next G-day	4 days max.
No action by Review Board	24 hrs max.

Similar problems are present when a new part is introduced in a company. Figure 3.3 shows an example of the data and process flow for the creation of a new part parameter. This is a good example of what is typical in medium and large size corporations for cycle time. Once again, the impact on this is trustworthy and timely data coupled with good processes.

The tool portion of the Figure 3.3 describes a process where multiple data builders feed a certain type of data. If roles and responsibilities are not clear in terms of a data and process owner, the set up and approval time takes longer.

In this example for a test yield in a semiconductor operation, there does not seem to be control on the other parallel processes in motion. Another level of complexity is due to location problems resulting in time zone coordination difficulty.

An error in one system can impact other systems which can, in turn, affect even more systems. This can be viewed as a ripple effect. As the size of a ripple effect error increases, so does the cost of correcting that error.

3.5 APPROVAL PROCESSES

Another factor in a new part set up process is the notion of approval. Figure 3.3 describes types of problems and the impact of the approval process. When an approver is not available, there should be a process in place for approval delegation. The authors have found that approval delegation is not done well in most corporations, potentially resulting in factory "line down" situations or product not reaching the customer on the promised target date.

Data and process problems can result in losing a good customer. Instead of continuously architecting a data solution, it is better to put in place an architectural roadmap of the operation. This will help identify root cause and focus an organization on fixing the very foundation of the data and process value chain. Figures 3.1, 3.2 and 3.3 can be used to replicate flows in most corporations and we would encourage you to take this approach. This will impact your customer retention models in a positive way.

3.6 DATA: THE HIDDEN CAUSE OF IT PROJECT FAILURES

Even if you were a betting person you would not like the odds of having a successful IT project in a medium to large cooperation. In a 1997 survey conducted by KPMG Canada[17], over 60% of IT projects were deemed to have been failures. There is little evidence that the percentages have improved since then. There are many factors that can lead to IT project failure but largely the data factor is not addressed or is ignored all together, resulting in a significant number of failed IT projects.

Chances are you have experienced IT project failures in your career as either a projects client or IT professional. Why do IT projects fail when so much effort is expended on their success? Presumably the clients knew what they

[17] KPMG Consulting is now known as BearingPoint . For more information about BearingPoint , visit their web site at: http://www.bearingpoint.com/.

wanted and were able to communicate the requirements. The IT business analysts were adept at working with clients to understand the processes and requirements and were skilled at communicating them as functional and technical specifications. The developers did their jobs and a rigorous and successful set of unit, system, integration and client acceptance testing was performed; and all this on time and within budget.

Well, if the project team was able to accomplish all this it must be a success, right? Not necessarily. If the underlying data that the automated processes are built to manipulate are suspect or bad, the users will blame the project team for an implementation they perceive as failed.

The ultimate measure of success for an IT project is in the perception of the end users, and if intermittent bad data is the output, the users will likely consider the best executed systems a failure to some degree. IT professionals can be heard to exclaim "It's not our fault. We automated the process just as specified in the requirements and the clients confirmed their functioning in testing". The bottom line is this: Can the results that the new system gives be fully trusted? Experienced end-users have an uncanny ability to know if the results are out of kilter. The accumulating flawed results are held up as evidence of another failed IT project.

One of the reasons the experienced end-user is so valuable to the success of an IT project is that he has been doing diving catches to get product out the door for eons. He has learned to intrinsically challenge the data and he has developed his own sub processes and checks that made him seem like a wizard to those who relied on them. So, did IT fail to identify these sub processes and checks? Were there data related missed requirements? If the robustness of the data input processes were not addressed then this was a miss, but if the accuracy of the legacy data was never addressed then bad data has claimed another IT project as victim.

Most IT projects discover the data problem while doing testing. The result is a likely delay in deployment while teams of individuals are utilized to correct the data. The authors have experienced that typical data caused project delays discovered at this late stage are 10% to 25% of the projects ultimate length and the result in cost over-runs and decreased return on investment. Many times however, the data problem is not discovered until after implementation or is ignored to meet project timelines resulting in significant post-implementation IT enhancements, data clean up efforts and end user and management ill-will.

Most data issues affecting IT projects can be categorized as bad data. That is, data that is incorrect or does not follow defined business rules. Bad data will require one or more techniques to be cleansed, discussed later in this book, but two other manifestations of the data problem in IT projects are missing data and purge data.

Missing data is usually the more serious of the two issues because it may be a hidden problem when converting from a manual to an automated process or when a wholesale change from a legacy system to the new system is executed. Missing data often requires the most resources to address because the data likely resides with many individuals in multiple formats and to varying degrees of quality.

In one effort that the authors are familiar with, complete and consistent bills of materials (BOM) were needed for the implementation of a Global Material Resource Planning (GMRP) system. Doing this required identifying the data owners for each BOM with subsequent interviews about what the universal BOM structure should be. The missing data effort required over number of individuals with many contractors added to complete the year long effort. This was a first pass attempt and required another year long effort after implementation to get to the level of goodness for the systems to be useful. The human effort was enormous as is the usual case when dealing with missing data. Well over half of the cost of implementation was attributed to the data readiness piece of the GMRP implementation.

Purging data is not usually as big a problem or effort, but understanding the need to address it in IT projects can have a substantial impact of the project's true return on investment. Purge data is simply data that should be deleted or archived and not bridged to the new system. It costs money to maintain data in terms of physical hardware and performance to systems and old purge able data has an uncanny way of getting re-incorporated causing degradation in the information mined from systems.

An all too common approach is to just get ALL the data into the new system. 'The clients will surely complete the purging of the data after the IT project'…WRONG! IT teams can make the mistake of trading expediency for value. The best time to address data purging is as part of the IT project or as a precursor to one, and although the result of not doing data purge may be minimal in comparison to missing or bad data, it may be significant and should be appropriately explored.

Whether the offender is bad data, missing data or purge data, all IT projects will need to address these IT project maiming culprits. If they are not dealt with directly in the planning of the IT project they will ultimately be addressed later at higher costs and result in delays and bad relations between management, IT and the client-end-users - another failed IT project.

3.7 DATA: A KEY FACTOR IN ERP PROJECT FAILURES

A special class of IT project failures is the Enterprise Resource Planning (ERP) failures. Because of its phenomenal cost and complexity, an ERP failure can potentially cause an entire company to fail. Successful ERP implementations must have a data strategy. Data readiness must not be relegated to a punch list item as explained further in Chapter 7. If it is, failure is a near certainty.

There has been much complaining in recent years about the dismal success rate of ERP implementations and no shortage of reasons offered as to why. Companies such as Hershey and Whirlpool have had very high profile failures[18], or some companies have actually gone out of business shortly after implementations. Much of the blame has been directed toward the big ERP software companies, but it is

---

[18] Wheatley, Malcolm. "ERP Training Stinks". CIO Magazine, 01 June 2000. http://www.cio.com/archive/060100_erp.html

now fairly evident that something else is going on. Actually many things must be done well to ensure a successful ERP implementations. Change readiness, training, process reengineering, stakeholder management, project management maturity, sponsorship, and the list goes on.

As with the smaller IT project failures ERP failures commonly have a data factor. In some cases it is the major factor, and also as with smaller IT project failures, it may be discovered too late. At Motorola's Semiconductor Product Sector (SPS) the authors experienced both failure and success in ERP implementations due to the data factor.

In the mid 1990's, one of the companies the authors benchmarked spent millions of dollars of an ERP program code named A. The IT work was exceptional and there was much hope in the results, but as the program moved into testing and deployment there were problems with user acceptance. The internal clients didn't trust the results and there was good reason not to. The underlying data was terrible. For years this company had been operated intentionally, entrepreneurially, as separate businesses and common data elements were anything but common, having different definitions, field sizes and business rules around their creation and management.

One example was the data element PDPW (Potential Die per Wafer), a parameter pertaining to the number of die on a wafer. It took several weeks to get consensus from the internal users as to whether the first 'P' in the acronym should be "predicted", "potential" or "possible" die per wafer. The separate user groups had legacy processes, each having a stake in which definition was standardized upon.

Which definition had the largest user base? Which definition would result in the smallest data cleanup and conversion efforts? Many factors went into the decision. Eventually, 'Potential' was the standard agreed to.

Other data elements required similar scrutiny, while still others were incomplete or had poor data processes associated with them. They had this big beautiful new system but it was like the Cadillac off the showroom floor with bad gas - no one wanted to ride.

At the end of the 1990s, Jan Harris, then vice president and director of Service and Logistics for Motorola SPS had the vision and foresight to create a team to address data directly in preparation for the next ERP attempt. This team became a center of excellence. Motorola is one of a few companies that can point to having had a truly successful implementation of SAP. Outside consultants attributed the ERP implementation's formal focus on data, and the techniques for doing so developed by the data team, as the primary success factors in the implementation.

It is common wisdom now-a-days that ERP implementations should not be thought of as big IT programs. Choose any of the big ERP packages you want – that isn't the most important decision. The big decision in order of importance should be:

- ERP or not?
- Is a big bang or phased approach correct?
- How do we ensure that all of the aspects of changing our enterprise are done in an integrated, understood and communicated way?

To the last bullet, realize that data readiness is the underlying, often ignored, success factor that must be planned for in order for any hope of victory.

CHAPTER RECAP

Information Technology (IT) initiatives and projects clearly require a solid foundation. As IT examines processes, implements enterprise systems, and collapses multiple systems of record, the underlying foundation is good data sets. This chapter introduced the notion of bad data, its impact and how it becomes a critical driver for the supply chain.

4 CHAPTER

COST OF DATA

INTRODUCTION

At the end of this activity, ask the participants that if they had a magic wand, what they would do differently. This information will help identify alternatives.

In most enterprise system implementations, it is difficult to justify why a company should make huge investments in a data cleanup activity. This chapter describes the use of activity-based analysis to identify the costs of bad data and good data. This is the most effective technique for determining the cost. To understand more about this technique, the authors have listed some recommended readings in the appendix.

4.1 COST OF DATA & ACTIVITY BASED MANAGEMENT

The first step in ascertaining the cost of data is to identify the activities associated in carrying out the relevant function. An activity is a task or series of tasks performed over a period of time. It is important to collect all the tasks associated with that particular activity including what is used like headcount, fixed assets, software, floor space, and any other factors that influence the cost. This will result in building an activity dictionary. The approach described in this chapter can be followed for any activity-based analysis and are not limited to cost of data only. This methodology is one way to extract from the analysis how much cost is attributed to bad data. Bad Data is any data that has significant adverse impact to the customers in terms of delivery and quality failures. Bad data also creates duplication of work and becomes a burden within the legacy or enterprise systems as discussed in later chapters. To get a good understanding of what it costs, it is necessary to carry out an activity-based analysis, a list of key and significant events or activities carried out to accomplish the function or work performed. This analysis is the first step for applying the following methodologies.

4.2 ACTIVITY-BASED COSTING

Activity-Based Costing is the use of software tools and methods to accurately determine the costs of products and services by accounting for people, machines, materials and overhead at the individual activity level. It is not a replacement of a company's financial reporting system. It adds management and operational reporting dimension to current financial reporting.

Feature - Assigns the costs of activities to the resulting products.
Benefit - Ability to accurately price products.
Feature - Identifies the relative cost of activities.
Benefit - Ability to identify low or non-value added activities.

4.3 ACTIVITY BASED MANAGEMENT

Activity Based Management (ABM) is the management of activities along with linking the outputs of ABC to factory modeling, cost driver analysis, performance metrics and Activity Based Budgeting to improve P & L [19] business performance.

Feature - Cost Awareness
Benefits **-** Improves awareness of resource costs, capacities, and utilization.
Measures the cost and performance of resources, activities, products and services
Feature - Understanding Costs
Benefits **-** Understand causal relationships between cost drivers and activities
Understand the impact of product life cycles and SBU[20] profitability.
Feature – Effective Cost Management

---

[19] Profit and loss
[20] Strategic business unit

Benefits - Support business decisions by developing cost models and tying them to performance measures and linking them to design decisions.
Support factory process improvement and cost reduction initiatives.

4.4 ACTIVITY BASED RESOURCE MANAGEMENT

Activity Based Resource Management is the process of identifying people activities, duration (time it takes to perform), inputs, outputs, performance measures, and cost drivers, then applying ABC methods to determine activity cost, and subsequently identifying and classifying the value/non-value added activities. This is similar to time and motion study the engineering community carries out.

Feature - Identifies what activities people do and why and for whom they do them.
Benefits - Ability to tie activities to goals, objectives, and customers, understanding the root cause (cost driver) for activities. This links performance measures against activities for effective measurement of an activity. This also drives dynamic changes through linkage of customer, output and cost while providing redirection or elimination of activities.

4.5 ACTIVITY BASED COST OF DATA

- Collect activities
- Identify percent of the total cost as cost of bad data

- Organize them against key processes
- Identify the amount of time spent
- Determine Value vs. Non-Value added activities
- Establish cost methods
- Cost out activities

4.6 BILL OF MATERIAL CLEANUP

When implementing an enterprise system, one of the first modules implemented is the one that contains a Bill of Material.

Here are some key activities to consider when cleaning up a Bill of Material:

- Clean up
- Populate Data
- Data Purge
- Data Metrics Preparation
- Routings Attachment
- Data Preparation
- Data Partitioning

The cost of these efforts can be determined by identifying various cost buckets.

The multiplier to calculate cost can be the percentage of time spent on the activity or other factors. Here is an example of a data cleanup cost can be calculated:

- Labor used in cleaning the data
- Cost of hardware for this effort

- Cost of any associated software for this effort
- Any other cost

In terms of a Bill of Material cleanup, if the data is bad, it has the following repercussions:

- Wrong parts being built or purchased
- Inability to build to customer specification
- Implications on ship date
- Errors on capacity estimates
- Impacts on planning for additional inventory to compensate for lack of trust
- Production delays
- Product being built or packaged in a wrong factory

4.7 ADDITIONAL CONSIDERATIONS

- Total level of effort in terms of hours and number of people engaged in the cleanup, tools and techniques used to populate data and purge the data. This means that instead of just calculating the targeted department cost for that activity, do not forget the other area's time spent on carrying out that activity.
- Methodology used, amount of effort that went into this methodology including identifying the methodology etc.
- Tools used, frequency of generation of metrics, number of refinement, etc.

It is very common to collect more activities rather than limiting them to a few.

But to keep the model simple, it is important to keep the activities to a vital few.

Most companies will go back to the model and identify the key business processes [21] so that the collection of activities[22] can be mapped to business process buckets. This makes costing and further analysis easier instead of following a commonly used term "analysis paralysis", i.e. over-analyzing the data and never getting to the cleanup.

4.8 NON-VALUE ADDED ACTIVITIES

In applying this concept of determining non-value added activities, a company will find some perceived Non-Value add activities. A non-value added activity is any activity that that can be reduced or changed or eliminated without deterioration of product or service and without jeopardizing the organizational existence

4.8.1 Examples

- E-mail overload
- Duplication of efforts
- Support activities with no customer value

---

[21] process = a combination of people, equipment, methods, materials, and environment that produces output, a given product or service. A process can involve any aspect of a business.

[22] activity = a task or series of tasks performed over a period of time.

- Meetings - Amount of unnecessary meeting time spent
- Training not to build relevant skills
- Redundant number of key strokes
- Time spent correcting bad data
- Troubleshooting and expediting all the time (elements of this can be Non-Value added)
- Excessive rework

It is important to identify non-value added activities for data, as they have a negative impact on the overall cost.

4.9 ALTERNATE ACTIVITY CLASSIFICATION

Sometimes using the word Non-Value add creates negative connotations. Some companies use the following classification instead of using the value add and Non-Value add buckets:

- Essential – What is directly tied to the internal/ external customer
- Necessary – Supporting the activities which are identified Essential
- Sustaining – Other support activities

4.10 RESOURCE DRIVER

A cost of activity is derived by using a unit of measure that is appropriate and directly tied in carrying out that particular activity e.g., time spent, tool time, equipment used, software used.

4.11 COST DRIVER

A cost driver is a factor that has a direct influence in the cost and performance of subsequent activities.

4.12 GROUP INTERVIEW PROCESS

One of the common ways of gathering data and calculating costs is the group interview process. This process takes into account participative interviewing that identifies what, why and for whom activities are performed. The merit of this approach is that this is very informal way of capturing all tasks and activities associated with that particular function. Also, as the target is to collect data from the knowledge workers who carry out this task, it provides a good snapshot in time.

By good facilitation, it is also easy to identify gaps and problem areas. Instances where a lot of time is spent on rework and number of key strokes spent due to bad data becomes more evident during the collection of activities.

4.12.1 Benefits

- Provides prioritization path for process mapping
- Ability to tie activities to strategies, objectives
- Understanding the root cause (cost driver) for activities

- Links performance measures against activities for effective measurement of an activity
- Drive dynamic changes through linkage of customer, supplier, output and cost
- Re-direction or elimination of activities

4.13 Gathering Activity Based Data

Here is the explanation of the process. The following supplies are needed:

Post-it notes -	Should be one color for each participant. If this is not possible, a combination of colored post-it notes and color pens may be used. 3″ X 3″ post-it notes work best. These are stuck on the wall by participants as they identify their activities per page.
Color pens -	1 pen per person.
Color dots -	These are self-adhesive dots, which are used to record the time taken per activity. There should be one color for each participant.
Large paper -	Used to put together all the processes on the wall as a permanent record so it can be taken back to the office as one document for typing
Scotch Tape	To keep the post it in place when paper is removed from the wall.

Excel Software - For loading the data collected. Identify a person upfront who will load the data and "crunch" the numbers.

4.13.1 Considerations

In many companies the process flow document at a high level may exist. If it does exist, use it to understand the department or area. The groupings of interviews should be a representation of similar area or processes.

It is better to collect data for less than fifteen people at a time. The duration for this exercise is typically four hours. The overall group should be a representative cross-section of the department.

4.13.2 Steps

The only part of data collection process that needs to be done by the facilitator is steps 1 to 12. For the rest of the steps through number 20, it is better to get one participant to write and another participant to ask questions.

1. Assemble the team in a conference room to allow all the participants freedom of movement.
2. Describe the project and the purpose for the project.
3. Distribute the pens and post it's to the participants
4. Ask the participants to describe the normal activities they do in the course of a week. One activity per post it note. It is not always easy to list activities within four hours. The best way to kick this off is to

ask them to remember what they did on the previous day and recap on what they were planning to do on that day and build on this. Every activity should have a verb and a noun. Activity is a thing they do in a normal day/week. Do not try to capture activities which take less than 15 minutes a day or 5% per week. E- mail and communication activities should be broken down to tie to a major activity.

5. Give the team about one hour to work through this.
6. Challenge the activity descriptions to understand what they mean. Proper description of an activity is very important.
7. Ask questions around how much time is wasted due to waiting for some other activity to commence their work.
8. Ask the first participant to place his or her activity on the paper or board. These should be listed from top to bottom on the board or wall. This is a good time to reduce the list by eliminating similar activities.
9. Ask the second participant to carry on listing activities in the same order (top to bottom) if they are different from the first participant. If they are similar, then they should be listed horizontally matching the similar activity. It helps to get another participant to drive this as ownership will develop.
10. The grouping of similar activities will point out that there is a key process here. If there are any doubts on where some activities belong, place it on an

empty spot on the wall, to be sorted out later by the group to identify another key process.

11. Repeat this step until all the post-it notes are placed on the wall.
12. Once all the participants have stuck their post-it notes, get a consensus on the processes that best describes the collection of activities and sub tasks. Validate with the group any more similarities or redundancies to limit the list to 20.
13. The group should determine what the relationship of a cluster of various activities to line up against a process.
14. Now we have a list of processes to work from.
15. Give each participant forty dots or more to use, based on forty hours per week. Even if they work more than forty hours, limit this to forty hours. Each dot represents one hour of the time per week. Ask the participants to place appropriate number of dots on the activity post-it to represent the number of hours spent per week spent performing that activity. Every activity may not end up with a dot. If the participants find it difficult to apply dots, ask them to build this from the highest time spent on an activity first, followed by the lowest time.
16. Count the total number of dots for each activity and record them for analysis against the processes. The number of dots collected per activity is converted to percentage of time later on for costing.
17. Now start working from the process sheet.

18. Ask one person to take a lead on identifying inputs to the processes.
19. Input is the event, transaction or requirement that initiates the activity. It may include a request from customer or a step required to start an activity, or the job description. Questions need to be asked around who, what, and what process triggers the activity. This will point out any process problems from the receiving end.
20. Identify the output of the process. The output is the product, service, information or transaction that results from performing the activities. It is the end result of completing the activity.
21. Identify the customer for each of the activities. When listing customers, if possible, collect specific names of individuals or departments who receive the outputs. Interviews with these customers can be carried out later to understand how the customers use and value the outputs. The output can also be linked to the departmental goals.
22. Identify the dependencies for each of the activities. Who or what is the activity dependent on other than the person carrying out the activity. Dependencies can be information, products and services from other departments or external sources used to carry out the activity in question.
23. Identify the cost drivers for each of the activities. Who or what impacts the cost of the activity. A cost driver is any factor that influences the cost of

performing an activity. It could be volume related, quality, and process driven or time driven.

24. Identify the performance measure for the output of the activity. What is the performance measure for the output of the process? A performance measure is an indicator of the work performed and the results achieved for the activity or organization. It should be a quantifiable and actionable measure of how well an activity was performed. These could be financial or non-financial. In many areas this may not exist.
25. Once all this data is collected ask the team to validate and finalize it.
26. Ask questions on what could change – like if this was your company what would you do differently to promote effectiveness and/or to reduce cost. These ideas should be documented and shown to upper management. The collection of these ideas can either tie to the process or can be captured as a separate exercise. Try to list ideas against individual processes.

4.13.3 Data Analysis

Once collected, the data can be analyzed in the following way:

- Convert the total time into percentage equivalent by adding dots.

- Tabulate the complete activity list with the percentages.
- Combine or drop the activities with less than 5% of the total time to present the data that will be used in the ABC model.
- Carry out costing of activities by working with the analyst or accountant for that group.

4.13.4 Examination

- Monitor high cost activities and processes. Match them against goals and objectives to ensure if they are lined up properly from the perspective of effort put into the activities, e.g., the highest-ranking goal may carry a 30% weighting factor and the matching activity may show 10% of departmental effort.
- Look for activities, which are not connected to goals.
- Look for cost drivers that are repeated for activities. Elimination of these or minimizing the impact of drivers, may affect multiple activities. Most groups will select ten cost drivers, which impact the most time consuming activities to work on.
- Look for activities with missing information like inputs, outputs etc. Some of these may not be needed.
- In most cases, get specific feedback against output of critical activities.
- Identify if there is a critical activity missing.
- Analyze if an activity can be done somewhere else. Do the right core competencies exist to perform the

activities or should they be done somewhere else, or outsourced.

- For activities where there are internal customers in the same area, there could be duplications of functions.

4.13.5 Charting Strategic Findings

The strategy chart should be compiled with the manager. On the left hand side list the processes, % of time and Activity Based Cost. The columns are:

- Monthly Cost – High, Medium or Low. High means, should the cost be higher, low indicated if the cost should be less.
- Contributes to goal # - Here we tie the goals to the process. This helps the determination of the weighting factor of goals against critical processes.
- Activity Status where G = growing in terms of perceived future need, S = steady in terms of perceived future need, and D = decreasing for future need.
- External Customer Feedback where E = essential to customers, N = necessary and supporting the essential activities, U = not either of the above (probably unnecessary).
- Does core competency exist within the group - Yes if it does, No if it does not.

- Can this be done somewhere else – Yes if it can be, No if it cannot be.
- Modify, outsource or eliminate this process (M, O or E).
- Management Readiness Factor – Is management ready to make this change (Yes or No)?

Once this is compiled, it becomes easier to identify what is the cost of Non-Value add activities, or which activities are barrier to quality improvements.

The analysis also shows non customer centric activities. This kind of analysis can be done without calculating the cost of the activities but the cost brings another dimension and it becomes easier to articulate to management, how many dollars are wasted.

4.14 Cost of Bad Data

Once an activity based analysis is performed, here is an example of how to carry out the impact analysis by identifying what the cost of perceived Non-Value added activities is and activities that have been impacted due to bad data. Now the amount of total cost of bad data by activities can be segregated.

The left column indicates systems used. The second column tracks number of transactions and per week against those systems in extracting the data. The third column shows how many times this is done. The forth, fifth and sixth column shows how munch time is spent by the client (user) who receives the data. By using interviewing techniques explained above, the percentage of time the client spends on working with bad data is identified.

The eighth column is for total time spent is the time spent by number of FTE in IT. The two columns following show how much time is spent on data and what proportion is for bad data. Once this is known, by using the resource driver, it is easy to calculate the cost of the activities against those systems in column 1.

The final column is the cost of bad data of the total cost.

For the authors in once company, it validated what companies have found that 17% of total IT cost is due to bad data. Such a data can result in a quantum leap in quality improvements as activities and their associated costs are known.

Figure 4.1: Cost of Bad Data

Applications	# of Transactions per week	# of Interactions per week	# of end users	Client time spent % spent on data	Client time spent % spent on bad data	# of IT FTE	Total time spent % spent on data	Total time spent % spent on bad data	Total Cost $	Cost of bad data $
CIM Systems										
System 1			1,000	10%	4%	20	30%	10%	9,332,224	3,016,489
System 2			1,000	10%	2%	20	30%	10%	8,663,726	16,584,000
Finance Systems										
System 1			100	10%	4%	1	10%	2%	713,000	281,600
System 2			100	10%	3%	1	10%	2%	713,000	211,500
System 3	7	37	1	1%	3%	1	1%	1%	6,700	2,630
System 4	54		10	50%	10%	2	10%	5%	370,000	77,000
										197,100
Planning Systems										
System 1	10,000		156	10%	1%	5	50%	25%	1,387,000	197,100
System 2	10,000		500	25%	3%	3	15%	7%	8,901,500	1,068,300
System 3	315,000	242,000	450	40%	4%	24	30%	10%	13,224,000	1,432,800
System 4	65	5,000	450	65%	1%	7	10%	2%	20,644,000	326,000
System 5	500,000		1,000	2%	1%	3	95%	5%	1,719,500	361,000
System 6	10,000	15	50	30%	4%	5	20%	4%	1,126,417	154,200
Operation										
A	60,830	115,577	2,500	4%	2%	8	40%	25%	8,749,092	3,670,000
B	4,000	1,000	200	0%	1%	6	1%	0%	120,042	141,200
C	140,000		1,400	5%	3%	2	30%	15%	5,482,204	2,977,200
D	700	35	4	30%	2%	1	80%	40%	260,000	36,000
E			200	10%	2%	10	3%	1%	10,771,340	533,227

4.14.1 Further analysis

More analysis, by now associating costs to activities, also showed:

- Error probability
- Reliability of the data activity
- Re-work due to bad data
- Cost impact of data within the process flow for that supply chain
- Impact on other areas who work with this area
- Impact of bad data eating away the anticipated return on investment for Information Technology and Information Quality budgets
- People productivity
- Identification of multiple systems of record, all using the same data – need to collapse, retire, after finding out that data is common to all
- Potential for saving cycle time based on down stream multiple systems now migrated to one
- That the cost can be used for outsource decision on transaction based activities

4.14.2 Bill of Material Data

The following example is quite common to a capital intensive industry for bill of material which shows errors as a percentage of total cost.

Figure 4.2: BOM Errors as a Percentage of Total Cost

Data Element	% of cost	# of Errors Fixed	Errors as % of Cost
Bonding Diagram	3%	37080	2%
Package Kit	10%	8225	36%
Cycle Time, Yield	85%	462430	22%
Routing	2%	2133	40%

The column describing the errors as a % of cost is derived by the authors' experience of implementing Bill of Material cleanup projects.

The above example is very common in many industries. Yet again without showing financial numbers to management, it is very difficult to communicate the value of an effort to drive costs down by data readiness and cleanup. These costs have a huge bearing on revenue and the bottom line.

4.15 IT CONSIDERATIONS

In the information technology areas most companies are using the SEI (Software Engineering Institute[23]) standards. One company carried out activity-based analysis and then matched them to the SEI list of activities to identify gaps.

The SEI list of activities shows the level of maturity an organization can attain, level five rating being the highest.

---

[23] Carnegie Mellon Software Engineering Institute, http://www.sei.cmu.edu/

The following is an example of the use of activity-based data to line up against the SEI model to identify the alignment of the current organization.

Figure 4.3: SEI Linkage Compared to IT Work Breakdown Structure

Capability Maturity Model (CMM) and ABM comparison

X- ABC Assessment found activity here

Requirements Management
Software Project Planning
Software Project Tracking and Oversight
Software Subcontract Management
Software Quality Assurance
Software Configuration Management
Organization Process Focus
Organization Process Definition
Training Program
Integrated Software Management
Software Product Engineering
Intergroup Coordination

	Not in CMM		evel	Level 2- Repeatable					Level 3- Defined								Leve
Activity	*% MSD Time*			*RM*	*SPP*	*PTO*	*SSM*	*SQA*	*SCM*	*OPF*	*OPD*	*TP*	*ISM*	*SPE*	*IC*	*PR*	*QPM*
Technical Work	16													X			
Standards- Coord., Write, Prod	14.5																
New Project Definition	12			X													
Roadshows and MC Outreach	8.5	X															
Tracking Supplier Progress	7.4						X										
Training	7.4											X					
Project Tracking and Overview	7					X											
E-mail and Phone mail Commur	6.7		X														
Writing Statements of Work	3.24			X			X										
Tech Transfer Report Writing	2.8													X			
Communicate with "My" MC	2.8	X															
Assit other Internal Projects	2.6														X		
Administrative Work	0.81	X															

The work breakdown structure in IT was analyzed by using activity-based analysis. This was then compared to the levels of maturity as shown on the template, like requirement management, software project planning etc.

First of all, by comparing this, it was noted that most of the activities were performed at level 1 and 2 and some at level 3. There were no activities at level 4.

The organization had a lot of work to do to get to the next levels.

The output also showed some redundant activities which did not match, and gaps where activities were needed. For example the amount of technical work performed on the x axis, 1.6%, may not be sufficient to meet the requirement management criteria on the y axis. Or the amount of time spent on tracking supplier progress on the x axis, may be excessive to line up against software configuration management on the y axis.

The notion of finding gaps and the identification of activities which have no alignment to any levels of maturity are clearly the target for further analysis. The charting can also be used for maturing the IT organization to the next level.

This can systematically be used for implementing development practices that continuously improve software quality. This can give a quantum leap to data quality activities.

CHAPTER RECAP

The whole notion of Activity-Based Analysis can be applied for group interview techniques. Many of the following techniques are taken from the book by John Miller.[24]

The use of the techniques discussed in this chapter can help substantiate or endorse any type project from the

---

[24] Miller, John A. Implementing Activity Based Management in Daily Operations. John Wiley & Sons, 1995.

perspective of Return On Investment as it applies cost to tasks, activities and processes used for that project.

The cost of output brings focus in terms of what to prioritize. The cost of bad data and processes stay hidden unless we apply the above techniques. Larry English's research [25] has pointed out that these costs are hidden everywhere and as much as 25% of the cost of an Information Technology area is due to bad data. ABC is a great enabler to point this out and can be used for value proposition.

In conclusion, the use of activity based analysis to identify costs will bring a new focus in terms of minimizing the impact of the cost of bad data.

---

[25] English, Larry P. Improving Data Warehouse and Business Information Quality: Methods for Reducing Costs and Increasing Profits. John Wiley & Sons , 1999. Page 12.

5 CHAPTER

IMPROVING DATA QUALITY & PRIORITIZATION

INTRODUCTION

In the previous chapters we discussed the value of data and processes and their role in the supply chain, legacy systems and enterprise implications. This chapter now looks at prioritization for optimal value in quality and at meeting business goals. The authors discuss a mathematical model derived to best achieve that value and meet those goals.

5.1 FINDINGS

The notion of Information Quality is attracting a lot of attention. Information Quality is about understanding the quality of your data, the underlying processes and making continuous improvements for the good of the enterprise. Oil industries use a concept of computerized maintenance management system to control costs.

Industry experts for capital intensive companies are finding that up to 30% of the data is either missing, incomplete, or is not correct. This is a significant cost for a semiconductor industry where one equipment set could cost as much as $2.5 million. The embedded data carries a significant value. Many companies have started using Cost of Ownership models coupled with good data to measure equipment utilization.

The sheer quantity of data that must be created and maintained creates problems. Typical data quantity problems the authors have found include:

- A company can have hundreds of thousands of part numbers, most of which are not salable. Typically, salable part numbers receive more attention and, therefore, tend to be cleaner than non-salable part numbers.
- For companies in the semiconductor industry, it is not unusual to find more than ten thousand product lines.
- Over 10,000 documents per year can be generated.
- Hundreds of customers must be interacted with, each of whom may have multiple shipping contacts, billing contacts, and design contacts.
- Including work in process, there can be millions of inventory moves per year.
- With the focus on outsourcing of logistics, there are a significant number of location codes.
- Complex pricing structures can be created that contain any combination of many variables including quantities, time, etc.

In order to deal with these problems, companies can spend a great deal of time qualifying and re-qualifying data.

Companies are getting smarter and are taking more time in fixing the underlying data sets. This is becoming a prerequisite in the implementation of the enterprise systems.

Besides problems caused by massive quantities of data, the following data-oriented problems are also common in many corporations:

- Many duplicate and disparate databases exist. Each database requires its own support/development team, has its own usage processes, and supports its own functionality.
- Many platforms (e.g., IBM, VAX, Sun) exist. Each platform requires its own support/development team, has its own usage processes, and supports its own functionality.
- Overall data quality is poor which can cause people who do not trust the quality of existing data to create their own data. This reduces personnel productivity.
- Inefficient data creation and/or maintenance processes which result in poor personnel productivity and unacceptably long delays before data is available for use by internal systems (e.g., manufacturing planning systems).
- Inadequate data processes and standards which result in one or more of the other problems listed in this chapter.
- Many data analysts required to obtain visibility to the entire enterprise data set. Without access to all

necessary data analysts, users may assume that data does not exist.

- Data incompleteness or incorrectness because people didn't want to use existing data processes, were not required to follow existing data processes, or were not forced to follow existing data processes.
- Spending large amounts of money on significant systems that use data (e.g., ERP systems) without understanding the overall cost and/or benefits.

Companies may attempt to address some or most of the above problems by installing web-enabled systems which keep track of metrics to create ownership of data elements in question. This is discussed further in Chapter 8. These work flow enabled systems are easy to operate and design. Some estimates show that as much as 75% of staff's time is spent in finding and accessing data. This is due to the fact the data is not stored correctly in the first place.

Larry English [26] writes that Information Quality has two components:

- Inherent Information Quality – simply stated as data accuracy. This is the degree to which data accuracy reflects the real-world object that the data represents (e.g., date of birth).
- Pragmatic Information Quality – the degree of usefulness and value data has to support the

---

[26] Larry P. English, Improving Data Warehouse and Business Information Quality, John Wiley & Sons, Inc.

enterprise processes that enable accomplishing enterprise objectives e.g. ACT score.

Data plays a major role in all six sigma quality initiatives. The transition in thinking for improving the cost of quality is depicted in Figures 5.1 and 5.2.

5.2 COST OF QUALITY

Figure 5.1: Old View of Cost of Quality

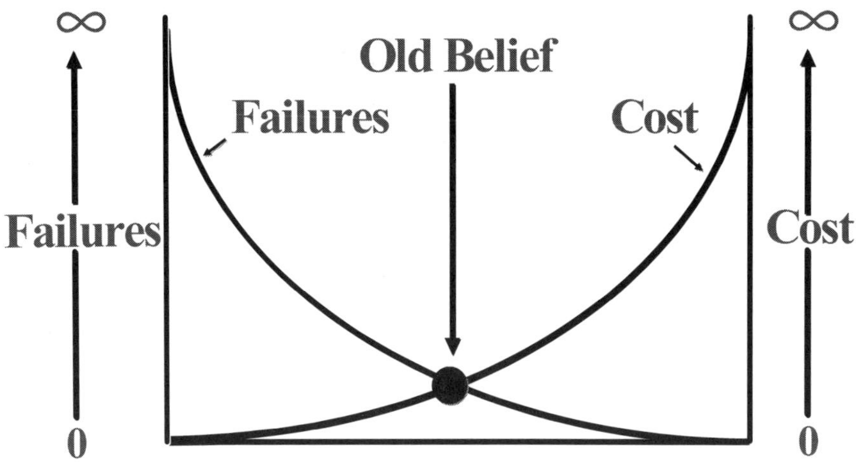

Figure 5.1 illustrates the old view that in order to improve quality, cost increases to an "optimum" point after which it's too expensive to get incremental quality gains.

Figure 5.2: New View of Cost of Quality

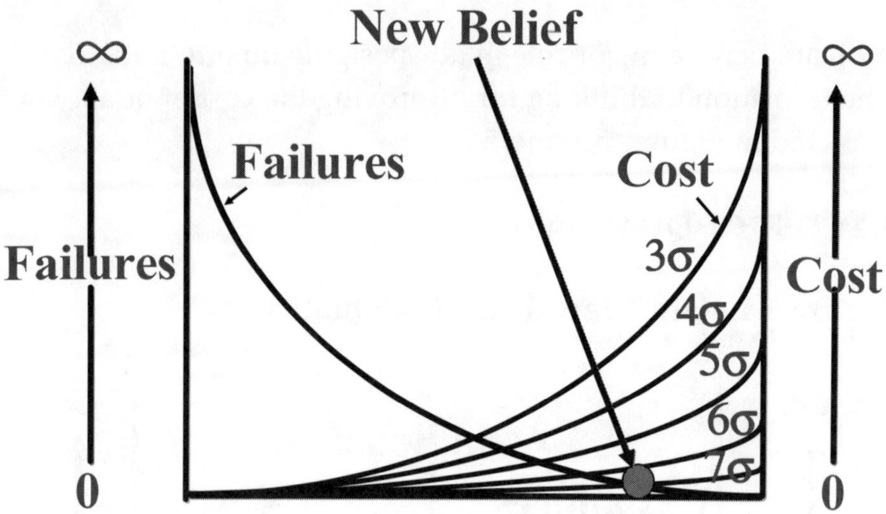

It also shows that as we increase our quality via six sigma methods, we can drive the quality to much higher levels at lower costs as sigma increases. This is the power of using six sigma methods for the data quality improvements.

It further emphasizes the fact that to achieve real value, it is essential to fix the goodness (sigma) of core data. The authors will discuss methodology and approach to this idea in later chapters.

The concept of looking at data has a new meaning. As discussed previously, the cost of data plays a significant role.

5.3 PRIORITIZATION OF DATA READINESS OPPORTUNITIES

When an enterprise comes to understand the pervasive need to address bad data, it can be overwhelming. Our experience at Motorola was like that. We had put together a formidable team and were engaged on multiple fronts in simultaneous data readiness, data process and system reengineering efforts. The more data domains we explored, the more we realized that what we thought was a data mountain to conquer was, in reality, a data mountain range. It was imperative that the limited resources we had should be used to scale the most important data mountains.

A simple but effective method for prioritizing data opportunities across multiple domains is through the use of what we call the Priority Cube Method.

Figure 5.3: Priority Cube

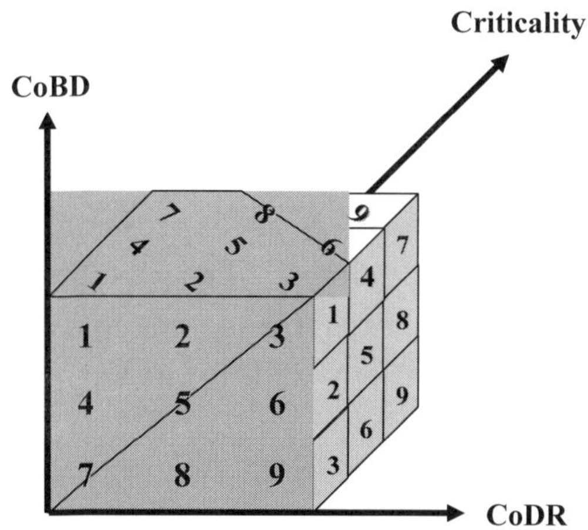

The Priority Cube places opportunities into a three dimensional grid space, based on the relative values to three independent factors. The position of an opportunity in the Priority Cube, or its numeric equivalent, establishes the priority of one opportunity to others across domains in the enterprise. To explain the use of the cube, we will first explain the three coordinates, then three comparative faces of the cube, and finally the resulting cube itself.

One could argue that there are only two dimensions to the Priority Cube, not three, because we are in reality weighing an opportunity against its Return on Investment (ROI), or business benefit, and criticality or business goals. But we break down the ROI face to its constituent dimensions. These dimensions are the Cost of Bad Data (CoBD) and the Cost of Data Readiness (CoDR): the third dimension is Criticality.

Consideration

When addressing prioritization of data projects, the following basic formula can be used:

Priority = Business Benefit * Business Goal

Here, "Business Benefit" is an expression of ROI (return on investment) and "Business Goal" is an expression of criticality. Users can quantify these concepts using whatever method works best for them, as long as this method is used consistently.

Using these definitions, we see that:

Priority = ROI * Criticality

Using the concepts shown in the Priority Cube, this can be rewritten as:

Priority = CoBD * CoDR * Criticality

Cost of Data Readiness -

Cost of Data Readiness is the cost of making the data "clean". This is not a one-time effort. The costs to purge, rationalize, create, convert or otherwise make the data ready must be taken into account. Established project management costing methods are most often used to get a cost per datum.

Figure 5.4: Cost of Data Readiness

$$CoDR = \frac{EffortCost(\$)}{NumberofDataElements}$$

Cost of Bad Data is a little more challenging to determine. It is defined as the cost incurred by the enterprise per datum if the data type is "bad" for a given period of time (usually the estimated length of the clean up effort or annual cost).

Figure 5.5: Cost of Bad Data

$$CoBD = \frac{BadDataCost(\$)}{NumberofDataElements}$$

The aggregate of bad data costs is calculated over the whole collection of the same data type. What is the cost of the cycle time, product number, piece part count, routing, specification, owner, etc., being incorrect? Historical information is a very good source from which to derive this costing information. Be sure to have the costing numbers reviewed by your finance group. Ideally, partner with your finance group to get values that will be defendable. Having folks from finance supporting your number is always a plus when arguing for project approvals.

Arriving at CoBD may require statistical techniques, but refrain from getting into analysis-paralysis. The Priority Cube Method is intended to be used with good, but not meticulous, analysis.

Unlike the quantitative CoBD and CoDR, the Criticality dimension is qualitative. Criticality is a measure of alignment to the enterprise's goals. We use a three tiered High, Medium and Low; Strong, Weak, Non Existent or other equally valid strata. In actual practice, we often qualitatively examine CoDR and CoBD for initial passes. When we do derive actual dollar costs we stratify the costs into High, Medium, and Low as well.

Now that the dimensions of CoDR, CoBD and Criticality are defined, let us look at three comparative faces of the Priority Cube.

Figure 5.6: CoDR versus CoBD in Value Analysis

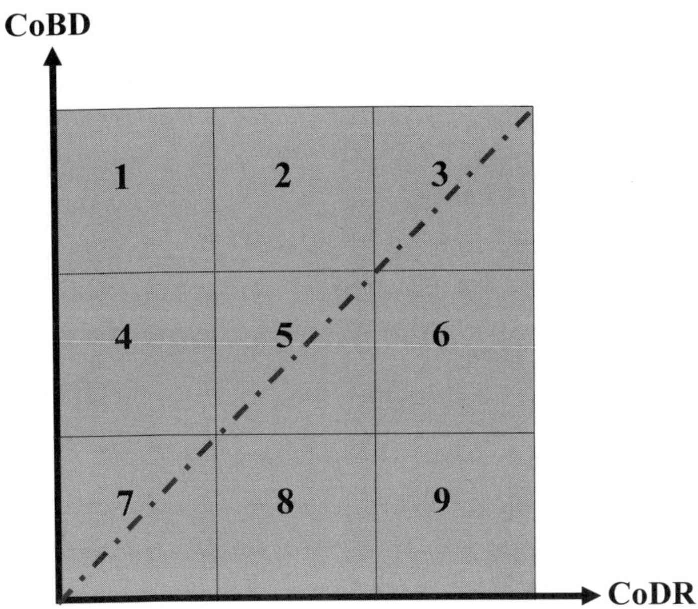

If the calculations are in dollars or relatively equal qualitative values, then any location above the 45 degree line represent a positive ROI. Because CoDR is a given and CoBD usually increases over time, it is essential that the period over which CoDR and CoBD are measured be the same.

CoDR versus Criticality and Criticality versus CoBD

For both analyses, the results are what you would expect, namely, data readiness projects identified as taking priority by management can have lower CoDR and higher CoBD compared to Criticality. The preferred / non-preferred line is shifted to indicate the comparative weight Criticality has. That is, projects that have higher correlation to the enterprises goals have a skewing effect and take precedence.

Figure 5.7: CoDR versus Criticality & Criticality versus CoBD

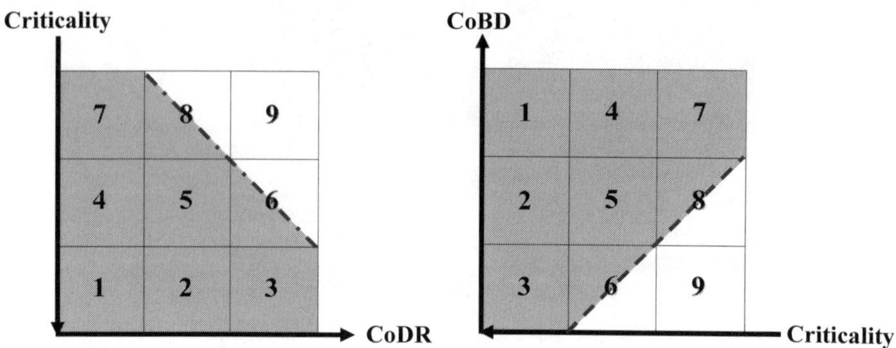

Finally, analysis of data readiness opportunities across domains is accomplished by its location in the cube, or more accurately, the location where the sub-cube of the three visible faces of the Priority Cube, or to the identified opportunity. This is a nice graphical way of presenting the project prioritizations but the same result can be sorted and illustrated in list form by deriving the product of the three coordinates.

Figure 5.8: Opportunity

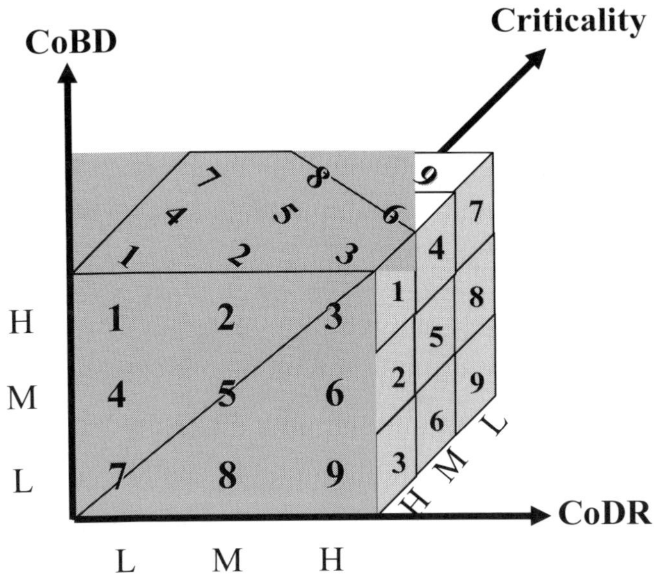

The Priority Cube Method is just one simple, but effective tool that can be used and modified to fit any company's potential data readiness project portfolio. If you have to determine the best approach to accomplish prioritization – congratulations! Your organization is sufficiently up the data culture maturity curve to be asking the right questions.

CHAPTER RECAP

Data quality trends have changed. Information quality plays a significant role in the quality of data and the cost of quality. The approach discussed in this chapter using the priority cube links performance criteria. Cost of data readiness must be understood. Once dollar values are applied, management endorsement is more easily acquired.

6 CHAPTER

DATA PROJECTS

INTRODUCTION

Companies often assess their data quality once a significant negative data event occurs. This may come in the form of a failed re-engineering program or an expensive data integrity error. These assessments often show that their data quality is far worse than expected and their first reaction is to immediately initiate programs to clean the data. It is from here that data projects are born.

6.1 DATA PROJECTS

Management should explore the opportunity to understand that projects can be much more than a data cleanup activity; they can be a chance to make significant changes in their data "assets" thus affecting the bottom line. What this means is that data projects should not be looked upon as a temporary fix, but as a chance to view how they can align data to support their company's strategy from a holistic viewpoint. This chapter was developed to help the business executive understand data issues that might be addressed during a data project outside of the actual cleanup activity. Later chapters will go into these issues in detail, but for now it is enough to think about data projects as a chance to create a new data culture.

Data projects, as with most projects, can be broken down into four phases: Opportunity, Planning, Execution and Closure. It is during these phases that the chance to make significant change in data culture decisions begins.

6.1.1 Opportunity

In the Opportunity phase, one of the most important issues that should be discussed is what data sets are included within the project and why. Many times there is an urge to go after all possible data sets (clean house), but what should be considered is how much this would cost the company versus the benefits.

Further chapters will touch on how to make this decision, but for now it is important to note that not all data are equal. Management should identify and concentrate on data sets that most closely align to the company's strategy.

This is really what can be considered the "low hanging fruit".

Another issue to address during this phase is sponsorship and resources. Countless data projects fail because the sponsorship of data projects is not sufficiently high enough for the cultural changes to take hold. The most successful projects support a company's strategy statement that includes the concept of data integrity. It is critical that the projects that support these strategies have executive sponsorship. Grass-root projects rarely succeed. In addition to the supporting sponsorship decision, a manager needs to assess their data resource expertise. They should first consider what in-house expertise exists. If it does not exist, they should consider contracting that expertise. If a business chooses to contract they must remember that a process must be put into place to grow the culture once that relevant expertise is gone.

One way to put that process in place is to include client representatives within the project. This will accomplish several things:

- First, by bringing in the "users" of the data the project manager will better understand the data's purpose.
- Second, many projects load their teams with technical experts who can map its flow through the data bases and applications, but have little experience with how the data is used. Without client support, the data may be cleaned up from a technical perspective but cannot have robust use for the company.
- Third, client representatives input and acceptance often translates to cultural acceptance. As a result, when the project ends, they will be the ambassadors of the culture, making sure that the changes made, remain intact, long after the projects are complete.
- Fourth, these clients will be your future in-house data experts. Once through the projects, they may be your project managers for future projects.

6.1.2 Planning

Within the Planning stage, it should be discussed how to define and measure the data. This is an important concept, as many companies define and measure data using technical definitions. While these definitions are needed so that the databases and applications can process the data, they often do not address what defines "good" or usable data for the enterprise. Data projects should include both a technical and a business definition of the data.

A technical data definition can be viewed as the definition that an information technology (IT) professional might use. This definition could include format, size, and units. A business data definition can be viewed as the definition that a data user (i.e., somebody that an IT profession might call a "client") might provide. This typically relates to how the data is used with respect to business processes.

This moves us to the subject of measurement. For the data projects to begin, they must develop baseline and on-going measurements of the bad data. By developing both the technical and the business definitions of the data, the teams can better formulate the requirements for the bad data measurements, and start the process of placing business rules around those definitions.

The concept of business rules is another issue which should be included within the data project. These rules provide the structure that will eventually become the data integrity culture. They should include the data roles (who owns, inputs, changes, deletes and approves the data), how the data will be stored and eventually will be the basis for the data processes per business rules.

6.1.3 Execution

Within the Execution phase is the notion of Data Stewardship. This is often confused with the role of data owner. An owner is the one in charge of the integrity of the data itself. A steward is one whose responsibility is the maintenance of the on-going integrity of a category of data element. This includes the processes and overall triggers of cleanliness of that category. This role is also useful when the data is shared between functional areas. An impartial party can guide the groups when disagreements arise. The concept of a steward, along with the customers of the data, can also be considered a possible candidate for the data ambassador to the company. The steward is one who monitors the data culture and continues to suggest improvements to management.

6.1.4 Closure

This moves us on to the Closure phase, in which the issue of on-going data integrity is addressed. How, once the data is cleaned up, can it remain so? Much of this will come from the data rules, data base and application changes, and processes and data stewardship. It should also include the communication of the data culture to the users and management. Change to a business culture should be presented in stages in which the clients are first informed of the changes (including why the changes are necessary), buy in from the clients, the day-to-day routine of performing those changes, and finally the on-going commitment from management that the change is necessary. This phase should outline how all of these actions will be in place once the project is complete.

6.1.5 Summary

In summary, there are many topics that should be included within a data project, outside of the cleanup activity.

These include:

- Choosing critical data sets
- Sponsorship
- Resource expertise
- Client buy-In
- Data definition
- Data measurement
- Business rules
- Data stewardship
- Culture change

By addressing all of these issues within a data project, the business has a far greater opportunity of creating a culture of data integrity that supports the strategies and goals of the company.

6.2 MANAGING DATA PROJECTS

Data projects are a unique opportunity for a company to address their data sets and transform it from an expensive liability into a competitive advantage.

In order to do this:

- Management needs to address not only the cleanliness of the data, but also what data sets they should address (knowing they have limited resources)
- Map how the data flows throughout the corporation
- Identify whether it is shared among functional groups and whether there are processes that directly address the data
- Decide if this equates into a culture within the organization that understands how to manage the data

We will attempt to address these subjects by offering real world suggestions on what to include in the data projects, as well as specific templates managers can use within their data projects.

Because corporations are now structured to be lean, they must balance the return of a data project against the costs. One way to do this is asking the question "What data sets are critical to my customers?" Depending on the type of business, the answers will probably be a mix of various scenarios. Some companies may point to the time it takes to deliver the product (cycle time) or the specifications from which the product is built (bill of material) or the cost of the product (cost of goods sold). What the manager needs to consider is what data element(s) aggregate are required to make up the element that is most important to the customer. This can be accomplished by brainstorming with various functional areas which will most probably name elements most important to that area. What the manager will find is that there will be interdependencies that affect several areas. These are the most likely candidates to begin your data project.

Once the elements are identified, the best way to estimate its current "data health" is to develop a template that has questions that cover the "who, what, where and how" of the element under consideration (Figure 6.1).

In the example template are categories of questions such as "what is the functional definition of that element". Although management might assume that all areas would have the same definition, the real world suggests otherwise.

The company in this example was trying to capture the definition of the element "Yield" within a data project. Engineering considered it an estimate of good product that would be the result of a particular process. Manufacturing stated that this was the actual number of parts. Planning stated it was an estimated number used to predict long term customer commitments, while the Finance area confirmed it was the actual number of good product that makes up the work in process inventory. It was obvious once the template was completed that engineering and planning were looking at the element "planned yield" while manufacturing and finance were looking at the element "actual yield". This

Figure 6.1: Data Gathering Templates

Functional Area: Manufacturing					
Element	**Element Definition**	**Data Base**	**Application**	**Is there a documented process?**	**What functional areas does the process touch**
Customer ship date	Defined as Date customer expects shipment	**Data Base A**	Application 1	N	M,S,P,D
On hand Inventory	Defined as Finished Goods inventory in shipping warehouse	**Data Base B**	Application 2	Y	P,F,MF,S
Yield	Defined as actual good product after test process	**Data Base C**	Application 3	N	P,F,E,D
Product specification range	Defined: Range of voltage that is assumed as "normal" within the manufacturing process	**Data Base B**	Application 1	Y	E,MF, M,D
Cycle time	Defined as days product is processed, from Assembly through Test process	**Data Base C**	Application 3	N	P,F,E,MF,D

	Roles: O= Originator I= Input U= User C=Changer D=Deletor							
Element	**Planning**	**Finance**	**Eng**	**Document Control**	**Marketing**	**Manfg**	**Feeds To:**	**Fed By:**
Customer ship date	O,C,D				I	U	Data Base C	
On hand Inventory	U	U			U	O,C,D,I		Data Base C
Yield	U	U	O,C,D	I		U	Data Base A/B	
Product specification range	U	U	O,C,D	I	U	U		Data Base C
Cycle time	U	U	O,C,D	I	U	U	Data Base B	

template proved to be indispensable in sorting out the differences.

Another category on the template is "what data base and application uses the element?". Many companies find that, depending on the area, there may be multiple repositories for the data. This is especially true of companies that do not have single ERP systems. The authors' experience with multiple data projects found it was not unusual for the repository to be as simple as "Bill's Desktop". This was a true sign that the data integrity was suspect, as people were so uncomfortable with the existing data that they made up their own repository. Once the information is collected within the template, a map of the "as is" data flow is the next step. An example of this is in Figure 6.2.

Figure 6.2: "As Is" System Map for Data Element "Yield"

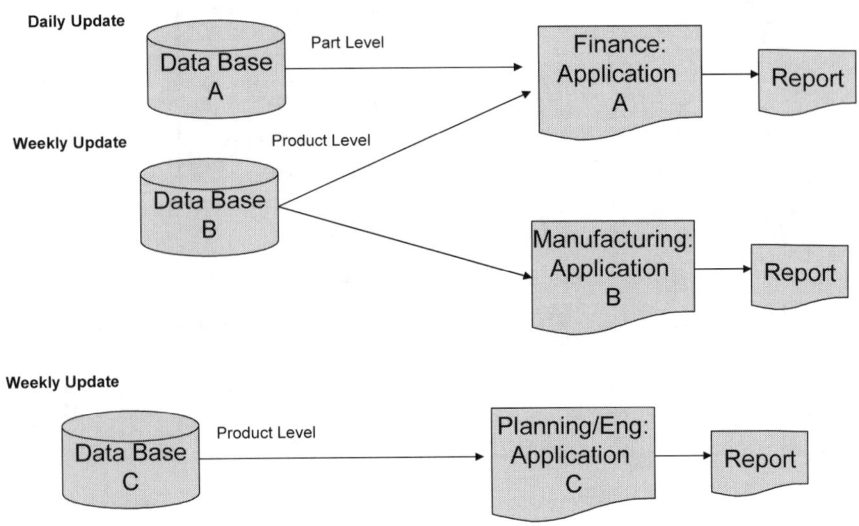

Included within this data map should be the databases, the applications they feed to and the timing of the feeds (from the database to the applications). Once the map is complete, it shows a complete picture of how the data feeds through the company. Managers often find at this time multiple databases feeding various applications to multiple functional areas. This is not unusual and is often the center of conflict when functional areas come together to discuss data issues. Each group brings its own report, pulled from its own database supporting its stance. Surprisingly, all areas are using the same element, loaded with different information. Ironically, everyone is right, using the data pulled from its own source. The data map is a helpful tool to help resolve these disconnects and overlaps.

Once the map is complete, the project team needs to consider what level of aggregation each functional group needs within its data sets. Manufacturing may need it at part level, while planning and finance may need it aggregated by customer or product type. This information should be recorded on the "as is" map and should prepare the team for the next step. The next step in the process is to develop the data "to be" map" Figure 6.3.

Figure 6.3: "To Be" System Map for Data Element "Yield"

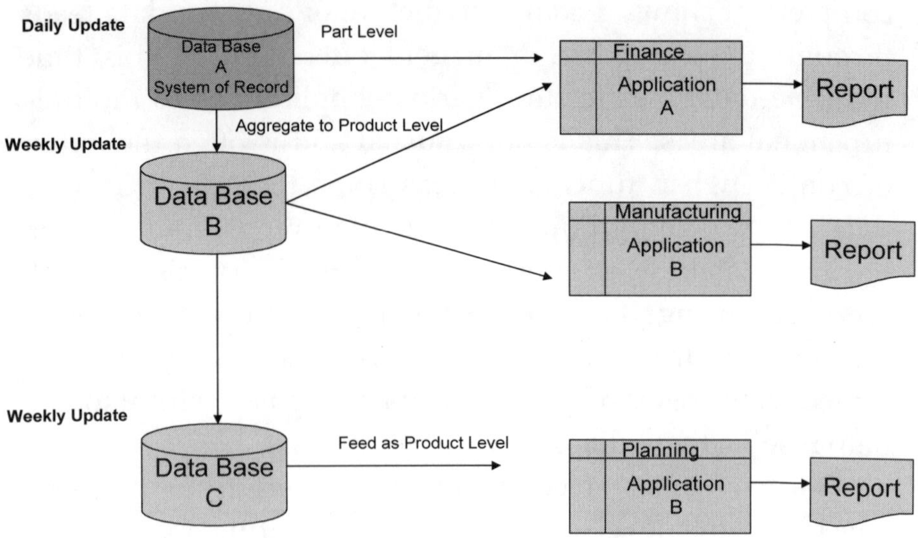

The "to be" map is how the group will link all systems, so that the data element has a single source from which all other systems are fed. This single source should also be the only entry point in which to add, change or delete the data. This single source is often called the system of record. One of the rules in picking the system of record is that it must hold the data at its lowest aggregation. In the case of the example, the lowest point is at part level. It must also be a system that is refreshed the most often. In the case of Figure 6.3, it is daily. Once the system of record is chosen, the Information Technology area will need to address all other system feeds by building feeds from the system of record down to the other systems. In these feeds, the aggregation and timing (according to the downstream system needs) occur. If the company does not wish to go through the exercise of connecting databases then they might want to consider changing their current systems to an Enterprise system (although an expensive alternative) which embraces the concept of a single point of entry.

The last category captured on Figure 6.1 is "who uses the data and in what capacity?".

This is broken down within the template as:

- Who inputs the data
- Who approves the data
- Who can change or delete the data and finally,
- Who uses the data

This information is used to establish the concept of data roles and is the foundation of data process and ownership. Although the map captured the "as is" process of the multiple databases and role owners, it is only after the system of record is chosen that the team can come together with the input of all functional areas and make the final role assignments. The authors have found in previous experiences that some areas will argue over role assignment on some elements while other elements may find themselves orphaned with no area wanting to take responsibility.

In order to overcome this situation, the project team must decide how the element is initiated. The initiator of the data should become the data owner. Other areas may have a large stake in what is input and would then become the data approver(s), while still other areas may wish to know that an element has been added/changed/deleted and would then be assigned the role as data stakeholder(s). Finally, in most cases, the group that inputs the data is assigned the role of data input. It is good to remember that less is better, meaning most areas only need to know a change has been made; they do not necessarily need to sign off or approve the change.

The authors encourage project teams to add no more than three approver(s); otherwise the process will significantly slow down.

After the role assignment exercise, the project team should move to update the "to be" data map with the functional area's roles. This will allow the team to move to the next step, taking the "to be" map (Figure 6.3) and turning it into a data process. The process should include the areas and their specific role responsibilities, the system of record, the aggregation rules, the timing rules and the data rules.

Once the processes are put into place, the team can focus on the cleanup activities. The cleanup activities are now made easier because the team only needs to focus on the data within a single database. All other databases will be fed by the system of record. At this time, it is a good idea to go over the system of record's existing data with all functional areas to agree on any changes that need to occur before the cleanup activity begins.

The cleanup activity starts with the concept of a baseline metric. This is the measurement of the existing data against the definition of what is considered bad. The guidelines of data "badness" should come from the definition of the element.

Depending on the definition, bad could mean any of the following:

- The data are missing
- The data falls outside a specific range
- The data are an input at the wrong aggregation level

It is up to the team and the functional areas to decide on the data rules.

Once the rules are in place, the initial assessment should be made. This assessment is the baseline metric that includes the entire data set and that data that is considered bad. It is also here that most projects make a critical mistake. The mistake is to use the baseline metric as their guide to the cleanup activity. What they fail to do is to understand that although they now have a single point of entry, roles assigned and processes in place, there may still be gaps within the system. These gaps may be comprised of areas which are not familiar with the data problems or systems missing feeds or gaps in the process. If baseline metrics, which take an agreed snapshot in time with management, are used as a guide to data cleanliness, what often happens is that as fast as the team cleans the data someone else in the corporation is making it dirty.

In order to prevent this (and discover gaps in the systems and processes) the team should develop what is called an On-going metric (Figure 6.4).

Figure 6.4: Examples of On-Going Metrics for Data

Cycle Time							
New = repeats + devices that have become defects after (Date)							
Fixed = no longer listed as a defect							
Distinct Parts							
	WW28	**WW29**	**WW30**	**WW31**	**WW32**	**WW33**	**WW34**
New		406	84	159	123	32	150
Fixed		708	103	310	380	315	117
Total	**2,561**	**2,259**	**2,240**	**2,089**	**1,832**	**1,549**	**1,582**
Number of Defects							
	WW28	**WW29**	**WW30**	**WW31**	**WW32**	**WW33**	**WW34**
New		594	179	222	189	58	210
Fixed		923	244	332	640	374	199
Total	**3,220**	**2,891**	**2,826**	**2,716**	**2,265**	**1,949**	**1,960**
Cycle							
	WW28	**WW29**	**WW30**	**WW31**	**WW32**	**WW33**	**WW34**
Yield	**WW28**	**WW29**	**WW30**	**WW31**	**WW32**	**WW33**	**WW34**
Baseline Defects	7453	7453	6753	6006	5221	4367	3442
New Defects	0	100	20	40	3	2	2
Fixed	0	800	767	825	857	927	950
Total	7453	6753	6006	5221	4367	3442	2494

The On-going metric will take the initial baseline number and track (by time increments) defects occurring by the lowest aggregation (part number) and by defects. In the case of Figure 6.4, if at least one piece of the data is bad, the part is bad. In addition it lists how many defects (regardless of the part) exist. In the case of Yield, there could be four situations where the data was bad and the part could be breaking two of those rules.

Figure 6.4 also demonstrates that while the project team is hard at work cleaning the data, they have failed to address all the gaps such as baseline and new defects. This should prompt a team to go back and review the process and find where the gap is occurring, and fix it before continuing with the cleanup effort. The success criteria are when the category New Defects drops significantly. It is only then that the team should start to consider the concept of data stewardship, which is the next step in the process.

It has been found that often in data projects the idea of a data steward is misunderstood and pushback from the company occurs. Questions are asked as to "why do we need a steward, when we have a data owner role". The reason for this is that the focus of the steward is quite different from the focus of the data owner. The owner of data focuses on the integrity of a particular entry; they concentrate on making that entry free of data errors as prudent as possible. The data steward focuses on the integrity of an entire category of data, making sure that the data rules and definition reflect the true spirit of the data. In addition, the steward is often the impartial overseer of the data. This can be useful when data disputes erupt among functional groups. Lastly, the steward can be considered the company's ambassador of data culture, the one constantly looking for ways of improving the quality of the data.

CHAPTER RECAP

In summary, a data project is an opportunity to address data so that it becomes an asset to the company. This is done by focusing on data critical to its customers, identifying its functional meaning, mapping the flow, identifying its users and processes and aligning systems, people and processes. This chapter offers several templates and examples to help the manager consider what they would include (outside of only data cleanup) to achieve that goal.

7 CHAPTER

THE FIVE PILLARS APPROACH

INTRODUCTION

Once data quality initiatives and projects are launched, all relevant steps need to be followed. The authors have used five tactical elements to ensure that processes and ownerships are in place to sustain the methodology used. It is referred to as the five pillars approach.

7.1 THE FIVE PILLARS OF DATA

Out of the authors' years of involvement in various and sundry data related initiatives have come five essential elements - a holistic data approach for medium to large companies. We call these elements, the Five Pillars of Data and they are in Figure 7.1:

- Data Architecture
- Data Metrics
- Data Readiness
- Data Processes

- Data Stewardship

The following sections of this chapter will address each of the Five Pillars of Data in more detail. Just as there are biological mechanisms and processes to create, modify and maintain DNA within the cells of our body these pillars represent, by category, the business biology required for viability.

Figure 7.1: Five Pillars of Data

The visual image of a pillar, as an element of strength, is a fitting one. Each of the five data pillars adds a distinct and interdependent support to the aspiration of good data. Each pillar carries a different, but essential load, for if any of the pillars are removed, the result will be that this data aim will be weakened and, over time, the imbalance will result in a failure to meet the data objective of trustworthy, timely and seamless data in the enterprise.

7.1.1 Data Architecture

The data architecture pillar is the set of rules and practices that if implemented, enable a company's IT systems to most effectively support good data.

Data architecture includes developing and deploying data standards and models to ensuring trustworthy, timely, and seamless data. Good data architecture recognizes that the need for data in the enterprise will increase and that users require flexibility in how data is sourced, stored, mined, and shared.

Data architecture is an enabler to the other data pillars. A robust data architecture facilitates the creation of data related metrics, systemically prevents bad data practices that require data readiness efforts to fix, enables good data business processes rather than dictates them, and provides the tools to assign ownership, accountability and stewardship.

7.1.2 Data Metrics

The metric pillar is the mechanism to measure the health of the good data practices in the other pillars. Through judicious use of metrics, behaviors are aligned to first correct data, then catch data problems in real time, and finally prevent them, as the enterprise develops a data culture.

7.1.3 Data Readiness

The data readiness pillar represents the best practices necessary to make the enterprise's data ready for use. Data readiness is a proactive effort and is typically the first of the pillars to be implemented in a company.

There are four data readiness activity types:

- Data Purge
- Data Rationalization
- Data Creation
- Data Conversion

7.1.4 Data Processes

Business processes that support data are essential to sustainable good data in an increasingly automated environment. If the data processes pillar is not strengthened, the result will be repeats of costly data readiness efforts. Adherence to good data processes are what data metrics were designed to support.

7.1.5 Data Stewardship

The data stewardship pillar represents the set of best practices pertaining to ownership and accountability of data.

Data sets with unclear or non-existent ownership will be a breeding ground for data problems in the enterprise. Data stewardship goes beyond mere ownership to create a community around data sets and ultimately a data culture in the company.

Figure 7.2: Enterprise Approach

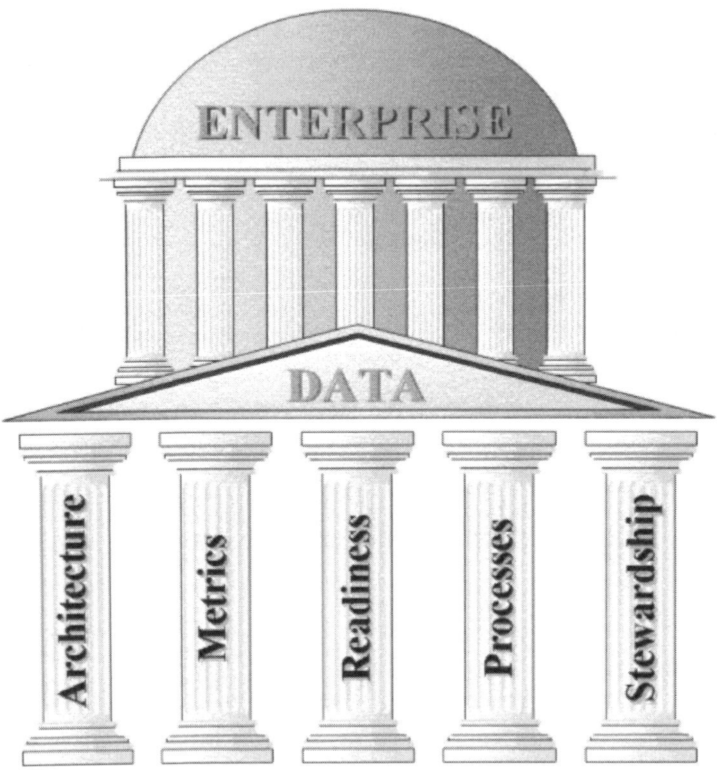

The five pillars of data are the essential elements to data becoming a company's second most important asset, after its employees. An enterprise's health is an aggregate of its good and bad decisions. These decisions are based on information, and, information is only possible if the enterprises data is trustworthy, timely and seamless.

7.2 DATA ARCHITECTURE

A carefully thought out and implemented data architecture can be either a blessing or a curse. If done well, architecture can make it possible to quickly and efficiently roll out new data uses and processes. If done poorly, architecture can become a bureaucracy.

Hint: If the only answer to the question "Why are we doing this?" is "Because that's what we were told to do", then whatever is being discussed may be bureaucratic.

7.2.1 Data Architecture Benefits

Effective data architecture provides a number of benefits. These benefits include the following, among others.

a. Architecture determines infrastructure. Infrastructure often dictates the data presentation method(s) that are available, both internal to the enterprise and with external trading partners.
b. Supports data reuse by ensuring that data is accessible.
c. Provides repeatable data processes.

7.2.2 Data Architecture Recommendations

When constructing a data architecture, it is helpful to keep the following recommendations in mind:

a. Keep the data supply chain short. In other words, try to avoid propagating data from one system to another to another etc. This is because:
    1. Every time data is propagated from one system to another, there is a delay. Delay can be problematic to downstream users of the data.
    2. Data that is stored in a system may be changed, even slightly, by the owners of that system. The system owner may not know how data changes will affect downstream users.

b. Ensure that each data element has a clearly identified owner.

c. Have a single system of record for each piece of data.

7.2.3 Single System of Record

It is sometimes viewed as expedient to enter data (e.g., product life cycle stage) into a manufacturing planning system and to enter the same data into an e-business system. Double data entry can be seen in the Figure 7.3.

Double data entry essentially doubles the amount of work required. It also introduces the possibility that somebody will type "gray" into one system and "grey" into the other system. While humans can understand that these two values mean the same thing, computers and systems cannot.

Figure 7.3: Double Data Entry

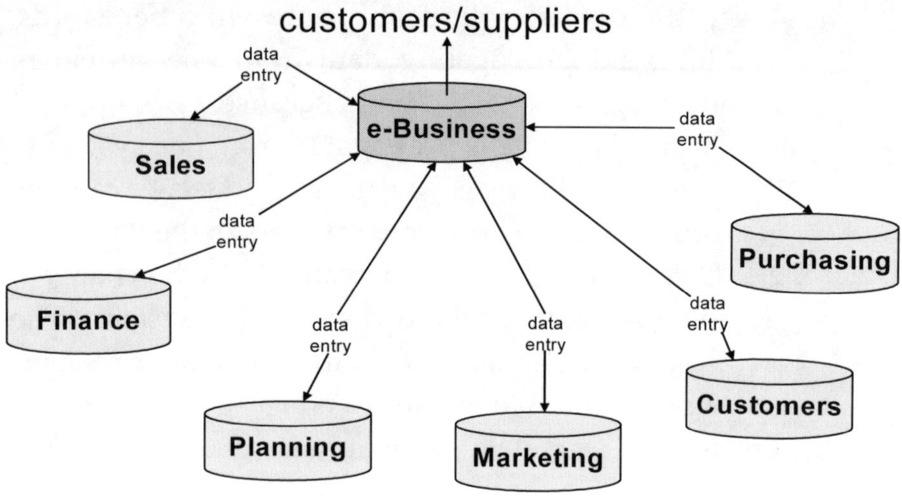

Entering data into a single system of record allows the same data to be used by other systems with no additional work. For an e-business application, the Figure 7.4 shows the benefits of having a single system of record.

Since not all data will have the same system of record, the data architecture must comprehend the need for systems of record that contain related data to be integrated.

Figure 7.4: Single System of Record

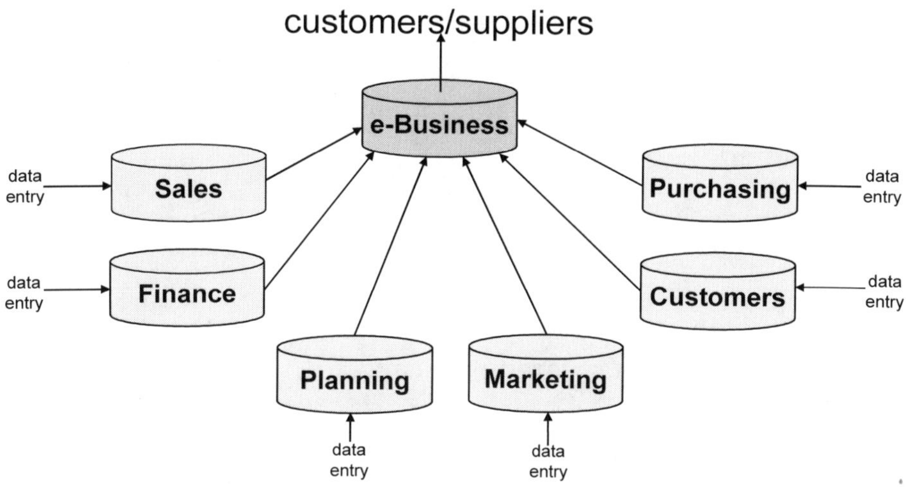

7.2.4 Avoiding Continual Data Cleanup

Failing to consider the above data architecture recommendations will usually result in a need to do one or both of the following:

a. Implement very sophisticated, and probably costly, systemic functionality.
b. Continually perform data cleanup.

The system functionality, referred to above, could include any of the following:

a. Web forms to enforce data quality rules.
b. Function-based (e.g., Marketing, Finance, Sales) approvals.

c. Mandatory periodic (e.g., quarterly, monthly) reviews of data quality.

While these functions are all helpful and beneficial, the cost of implementing and maintaining them must be considered.

7.2.5 Data Warehousing

Any data architecture must include the creation of a data warehouse. A data warehouse can:

a. Contain historical data. Often, a system of record will contain only current data. To perform many types of analyses (e.g., time-based trends), access to historical data is critical.
b. Bring data from multiple systems of record together. Often, business metrics require comparison and/or contrasting of data from different systems of record (e.g., customer shipments data from a logistics system and customer orders data from a sales order system). Having all needed data in a data warehouse makes it much simpler to created needed metrics than if the metrics creator also needed to create data feeds from all pertinent systems of record.

7.2.6 Zachman Framework

To provide a common vocabulary and methodology for discussing enterprise architecture (including data architecture), John Zachman developed the Zachman Framework. More information on the Zachman Framework can be found by consulting the Zachman Institute for Framework Advancement[27]. This framework has provided many companies a step by step approach to put together a good architectural roadmap.

7.3 DATA METRICS

Per Philip Crosby [28], Quality is Conformance to Requirements.

Information quality (IQ), per Larry English[1], is a function of:

- Quality Data
- Quality Definition
- Presentation Quality

Improper metrics will cause the organization to focus on the wrong thing;

Too Many Metrics Dilutes the Focus. *Less is More.*

In most companies, different departments have different metrics that can sub-optimize the total organization.

The value in Information Quality is to get these metrics to be used to promote action plans. Action can only be taken when something can be measured in a quantitative manner. As discussed in the introduction chapter, data fuels the

---

[27] http://www.zifa.com/

[28] Crosby, Philip B. Quality is Free: The Art of Making Quality Certain. Mentor Books, 1992.

enterprise. But data is seldom measured. Metrics drive behavior.

When the first data projects are launched, there is a tremendous amount of success in the cleanup and seamless transfer of data and processes into fewer systems of record and enterprise systems. What is very common is that this glory is short lived. The authors found that people break and corrupt data faster than the amount of data being fixed; hence, the notion of metrics.

Having metrics alone is not sufficient. It is important to endorse ownership of the metrics up front when fixing the data. The only way this works is if the measurement system is tied to the individual's performance measurement criteria. The authors refer to the notion of ownership as someone who is the Data Steward. This is discussed at the end of this chapter.

Once a determination of the ownership and data is made, metrics generation and tracking can be done.

The authors' work has been in the area of:

- Q Data = Trustworthy, Timely and Seamless.
- Q Definition = Clear and Understood.
- Q Presentation = Efficient and Effective.

Keeping the above in mind, there are three types of metrics:

- Quantitative and Qualitative
- Operational and Temporal
- Executive and Detailed

Metrics can further be broken into the following types:

- Sizing
- Trend charts
- Stoplight charts
- Completeness for the robustness of process or data
- Validity – automatic, manual
- Measurement of Accuracy
- Usability
- Pareto
- Histogram
- Statistical Process Control
- Timeliness
- Cost to get a measurement of value add in terms of cost and ROI

Data quality is achieved though people who have the visibility to know what needs to be fixed and then do it! Metrics tell us if they did or did not.

Figure 7.5 depicts data readiness metrics. The numbers of defects are tracked as critical and non-critical. Critical are those which stop a production line or end up impacting the end customers directly. Non-critical defects are those which have an impact on the overall supply chain, but do not impact productivity in an adverse manner.

The target is to bring the defect levels to a sustainable and acceptable level. It is not possible to bring this to zero due to timing difference, expediting products, or any special requirements prompting the corporation to get the product out for the customer. The initial objective is to bring the critical defects down as they impact customer on time delivery. The next step is to do a similar exercise for non-crucial defects.

Figure 7.5: Data Readiness Metrics

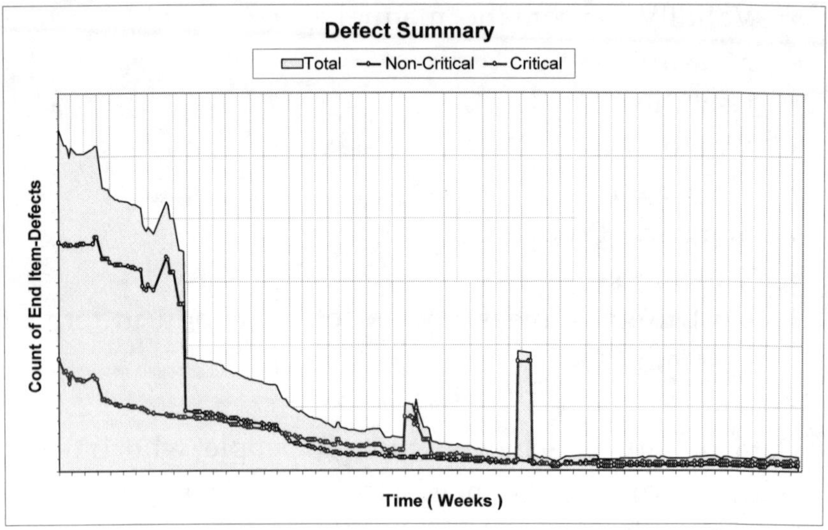

Figure 7.6 illustrates cycle time in number of days for transactions impacting output of product. The transaction cycle time is measured as the amount of days it takes to process a transaction for the product. Within the approval cycle, more time is added as every transaction has uniqueness and needs approval at the next level. The total cycle time is measured as start to close cycle time. Without dissecting the metrics into approval time and transaction processing time, the company can focus where the problems are.

Figure 7.6: Cycle Time Improvements

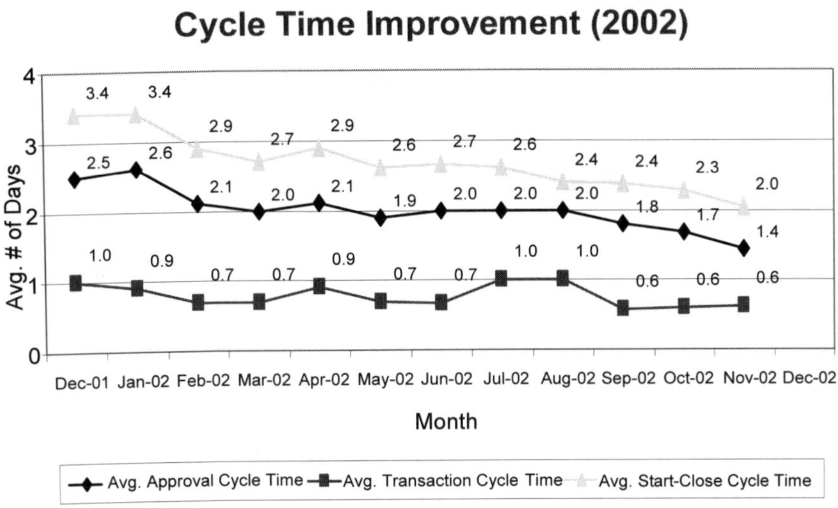

A benchmark number is to get the number of approvers to a few -like less than two. This will reduce the gap between approval time and transaction processing time.

The second measurement is of the business processes. These have to be measured in terms of Quality (Business Rules!), Cost (Systems & Activity), Time (Cycle Time), Process Capability (Six Sigma) and Usage (Transaction Volume & #Users).

- Define the Business Rules
- Measure the Data to the Rules (Daily)
- Identify All the Data Owners, Approvers, Stewards and Their Managers
- Send the Owners an E-mail Daily or Weekly With the Trigger or Data Defects That Need Their Attention
- Send the Individuals and the Managers the Metrics

Once the methodology on rules is identified, the authors have found that a unique identity, like rule number, is associated to the business rules. This helps design the metrics to show number of defects by rule number.

Figure 7.7: Pareto Chart

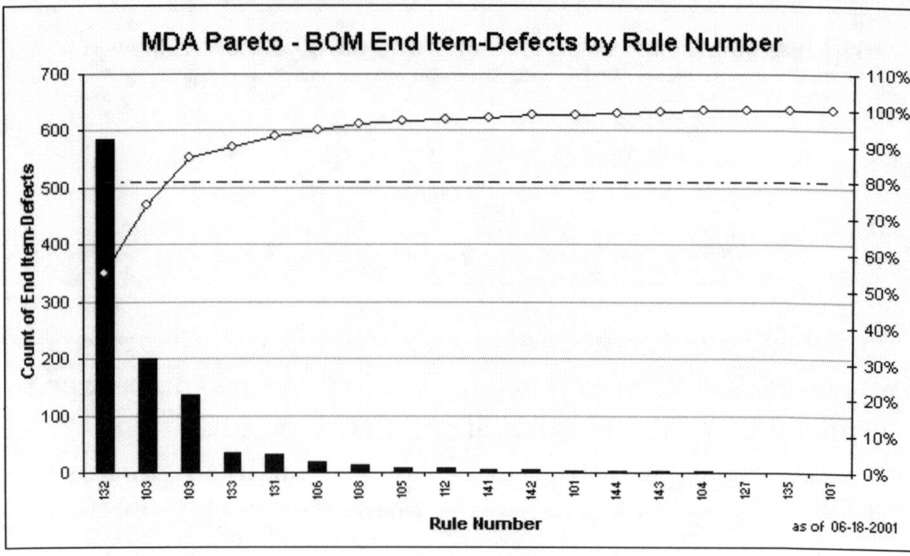

The above Pareto chart shows defects by rule numbers for a Bill of Material.

7.3.1 Metrics for ROI (Return on Investment)

Metrics helps communicate the Return on Investment in a quantifiable manner. Take an example of a planning system:

- Amount of time spend on populating and then correcting data fields which can involve Planning, Sales and Marketing and other areas
- Metrics will track impact on inefficiencies and impact on bad data
- ROI for collapsing systems – cycle time metrics plays a significant role here. Saving also on cycle time based on down-stream multiple systems, instead of on a few systems of record.
- People Productivity metrics - Easy access of data, better usage of capacity, reduce inventory to manage, easy to schedule in terms of parameters and factory on time delivery, mainly manufacturing

"The best thing we did was to identify the data metrics, make them easily reported on an individual basis, added data metrics to individual goals and review weekly (and publicly) in our individual planning staff meetings. Simple, clean and consistent feedback."

Feedback from a Planning Manger.

Metrics Drive Behavior, what Gets Measured Gets Done!

Metrics is a Key Success Factor for Information Quality.

7.4 DATA READINESS

Data Readiness, the first pillar of good data, is sometimes incorrectly called by another name, data cleanup; it can be divided into four types - Data Purge, Data Rationalization, Data Creation and Data Conversion. Data readiness can be defined as the activities necessary to make the enterprise's data ready for use. Understanding what data readiness is and in what forms it can be found are necessary to effectively address bad data.

Figure 7.8: Data Readiness

As stated earlier, an organization's first collision with large scale data problems is usually during an IT effort of some type. Maybe in testing a system the realization comes that things are not working correctly and bad data is discovered to be the culprit. The implementation is delayed and there is blame and finger pointing. Or, worse yet, the data problem is not discovered until after implementation and the business is impacted in one of several ways. Resources are then marshaled to correct the problem. This activity of correcting the data is often called data cleanup, but differs from data readiness in that data readiness is a proactive effort.

Data readiness involves defining, analyzing, planning and executing to ensure that data in the enterprise's systems are correct. Data readiness efforts should be formatted into projects because they have a defined scope and are time bound. Data readiness is not an on-going or re-occurring cleanup of a data set. If a data set is continually being readdressed and cleaned, then one or more of the other pillars of good data are not being followed.

Data purge is the act of removing or archiving data from systems of record in order to meet a readiness objective. As an enterprise replaces its legacy systems, one of the first steps will likely be the purging of data that no longer has relevance or business value. Data that is no longer relevant but still in systems of record puts undue burden on those systems' resources, increases the time of queries, and can lead to false statistical conclusions when data mining; it also requires maintenance and disk space.

Data purge is usually straight forward and doesn't require as great an investment in resources compared to the other data readiness types. In fact, it is a good practice to consider data purge opportunities before the other data readiness types are executed. This will likely save time and resources since this will result in doing data rationalization or data conversion on a smaller set due to a well thought out and executed data purge activity.

In preparation to do a large data conversion activity in support of an enterprise resource planning (ERP) core data implementation, Motorola reduced its material master records from near 500,000 individual records to less than 180,000 materials. The data purge activity reduced the projected CoDR (Cost of Data Readiness per datum) by over 50%. There are inherent risks to purging data, but these risks can be mitigated with planning, clear business rules, and data owner and client involvement.

In increasing levels of difficulty, Data Conversion is the next of the four data readiness types. Data conversion is the transformation of data to meet a data readiness objective. Data conversion is nearly always required when a new system replaces an old system. It may be as simple as rearranging the order of fields of a record into the new system or as complicated as converting large free form text strings into discrete fields that have strict data types and business rules.

Successful data conversions are those that invest the effort necessary to understand the existing data well enough to maximize the automation of legacy data conversion. 100% conversion automation is rarely achieved and shouldn't be the goal. There is a corresponding and increasing cost to automate more complex problems within a data set. The team that has paid the price to understand the legacy data will arrive at the correct balance of conversion automation versus manual conversion.

Data creation is the combining, deriving or manufacturing of data to meet a data readiness objective. A good example of data creation is in a Bill of Material population of a routing field where the routing does not exist. As with data conversion, the impetus of data creation is usually the implementation of a new IT system. The lines between data creation and conversion blur when a data set in a new system is a combination of data elements from the legacy systems. The reverse, the decomposition of a data element in the legacy system into multiple data elements in the new system, is clearly data conversion.

Derived data conversion activity implies that some logic is performed upon the legacy data that makes it a created or derived data set. For example, let's say that in a legacy system, manufacturing locations and routings are two distinct data elements but in the new system a data element, transportation lane, is required and it is a derived combination of the two legacy elements.

The most resource intensive form of data creation is data that is not presently in a system of record but needs to be in order to achieve data readiness. It could be data that exists on an individual data owner's desktop computer or, worse yet, in his or her head. An example of this might be parametric product data. Customers require more and more data about products - environment data, life cycle data, pricing and quantity data or product performance data. The types of data customers require are ever increasing and customers want it now and automated. Customers don't want to call a sales person and wait for him or her to get voltage values from the product engineer in a few days or even minutes. EDI (Electronic Data Interchange) and B2B (Business to Business) require companies to create data in systems of record where they can be managed and supplied as necessary.

The creation of data begins with an understanding of what the data will be used for, so that the appropriate system architecture can be created. Next, business rules pertaining to the data must be agreed upon and implemented in the system's interface, and finally the data must be created into the system of record. In some data readiness efforts the architecture and system are purchased, but the bulk of the effort is still ahead of the team - getting the data into the system. It is typical that when one is involved in a data creation data readiness effort, that business culture changes are afoot.

Culture changes, including data-culture changes are difficult. Data owners may be resistant to changing the way they have always handled the data. The resulting changes may mean more system control in order to assure configuration management; and let's be honest, (speaking directly,) data is power and some will be reticent to relinquish it. Even with cooperative data owners, data creation is largely manual and resource intensive.

Close in effort to data creation, but greater in complexity, is Data Rationalization. Data rationalization is the evaluation and improvement of data based on business rules in order to meet a data readiness objective. Data rationalization is data correction and can have elements of any or all of the other three data readiness types. It is a result of inadequate or poor adherence to data business rules pertaining to creation, modification and deletion.

The extent of the data rationalization effort is dependant on the quality of the data related business rules and the extent to which the data adheres to these rules. Data rationalization efforts should always begin with a comprehensive review of the data related business rules to ensure they are sufficient. The definition of sufficient here is that if the rules were followed, they would guarantee continued data readiness.

Data rationalization is usually a manual exercise because automation is dependant upon having measurable business rules. The poor quality and incompleteness of data involved in these efforts require record by record and field by field analysis by individuals that understand the associated business processes and can interpret intent. Rationalization often requires one-on-one interviews with data owners in order to be successful. Because of the time and effort, there may be resistance on the part of the data owners to data rationalization efforts.

Data rationalization efforts are usually carried out on an active system of record. Data is being created and modified while the team is attempting to rationalize it. An effort that begins to make data corrections before addressing the quality of the data related business rules will be wasted because the rules that lead to the bad data problem have not been corrected. Data rationalization efforts that work with data owners and data clients to arrive at measurable data business rules before the correction process begins will also benefit by having a set of clear yardsticks by which to rationalize the data against. Ideally, the rules will be digitized, or in other words, coded into the systems interface thus preventing future rule violations.

Data rationalization, creation, conversion and purging are activities that are required in all companies that have data systems. Well planned data readiness activities based on an understanding of the four data readiness effort types,

Figure 7.9: Types of Data Readiness

The Four Types of Data Readiness

Data Purge	Data purge is the act of removing or archiving data from systems of record in order to meet a readiness objective
Data Conversion	Data conversion is the transformation of data to meet a data readiness objective
Data Creation	Data creation is the combining, deriving or manufacture of data to meet a data readiness objective
Data Rationalization	Data rationalization is the evaluation and improvement of data to business rules in order to meet a data readiness objective

their relative complexities, effort level and approaches, will prevent unplanned data cleanup costs and delays in system implementations and increase the real and perceived success of data system related initiatives.

7.5 DATA PROCESSES

The authors emphasized the value of good data in the previous chapters. Good processes are augmented by good data. In the whole data thread, the data process plays a significant role from the perspective of input and outputs to the processes.

7.5.1 Achieving High Quality & Timeliness?

Through capable and repeatable data processes!

Data is captured, entered and maintained in systems and databases via a data process. Data processes are a specific type or part of a business process. Examples of data processes include capturing a customer's name and address, creating a bill of material for manufacturing, deleting a part number or changing a status code. Large enterprises have hundreds, if not thousands, of data tasks and processes. Each of them contains one or more steps. Examples of the steps in a data process for adding a new customer with credit terms may include:

1) Acquire or create the data content
2) Send the request to the data owner or whomever in the enterprise is allowed to start the data process
3) Data owner insures completeness and accuracy to a set of business rules and standards

4) The data is entered into the customer database
5) Obtain approval from manager
6) Obtain approval from Credit department
7) Activate the customer record.

Sometimes data processes are well defined and repeatable and sometimes they are ad-hoc. Sometimes the process produces high quality data and sometimes it does not. Either way, it's the process and the people who use it that determine whether or not it is capable of producing high quality data in a timely manner.

When the process is not capable of producing high quality data, eventually the data becomes dirty, and so painful to the business, that the crisis is recognized and a data cleanup team is formed! The problem is, that if the team does not fix the root cause problems in the process, the data from the cleanup task will need to be repeated again and again. Therefore, it is better to fix the process so the data is collected and processed correctly the first time.

In Philip Crosby's book Quality is Free,the point is made that it costs much more, in the long term, to do inspection and rework than it does to do design capable processes and do it right the first time.

Key Point: Cost of Rework > Cost of Fixing the Data Process

The nice thing about processes is that they can be measured, controlled, and improved. Measuring the data and the data process is required to determine whether the process is capable or not. The measurements for a data process include:

1) The quality of the data, does it meet or exceed specifications. For example, is the data set complete? Is it current? Is it accurate enough for the intended business use?
2) The processing time or cycle-time, how long does it take from the point in time the enterprise first has the knowledge, enters it into the "process" and the data is part of the database? Is it seconds, hours, days, weeks or even months? What does it need to be?
3) Cost: How much money does the enterprise spend to gather the data and process it so that it is available for decision support tools and other application or views. What is the benchmark?

The process capability is determined for each process goal such as quality, time or cost. A process may be capable of meeting one, but perhaps not all of the requirements. For example, the quality requirements may be met, but not the time requirements. All three should be measured.

Figure 7.10 highlights the frustration of silo management. It is typical in a corporation for the processes to be owned in a silo. As there is no integration, the interdependencies of processes do not exist. Therefore, if there is a failure in one area, the problems reappear somewhere else. With silo processes, metrics are difficult to enforce. The whole landscape of processes becomes difficult to maintain. Applications cannot be integrated seamlessly. It also creates the vast number of disparate owners and stakeholders, and cleanup becomes very complex.

Figure 7.10: Work Flow Problems

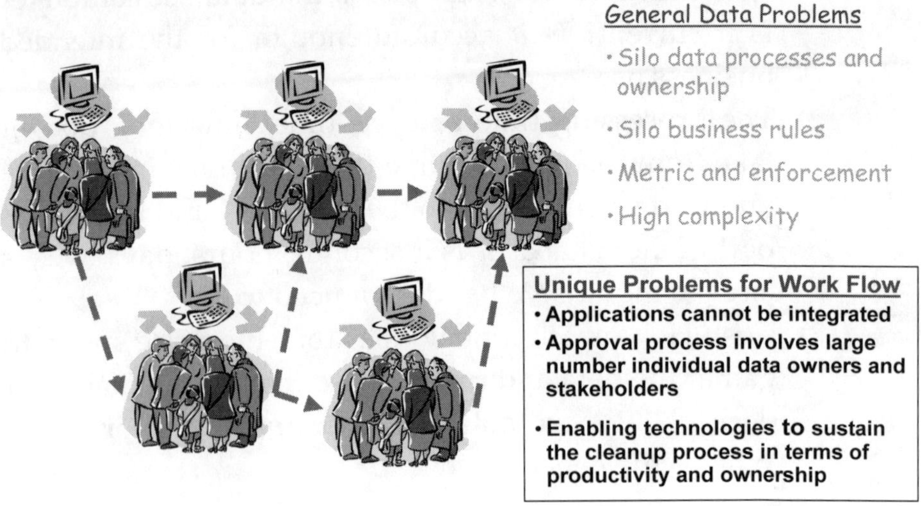

7.5.2 Elements of a Robust Work Process

- Documented and improved over time so that an active configuration management can be carried out
- Should have an input and output
- No more than two approval signatures
- Defined capacity and capability
- Can be linked to peoples' roles: Accountability!
- Easy to learn/use like Online Training
- Web Enabled
- Can be captured seamlessly
- Should have an approval and escalation criteria

- Maintainable
- Supports the business need: Capable
- Workflow Enabled: Repeatable
- Is the Only Way That "Business Need" Is Accomplished
- Timely, Responsive
- Quality Built in
- Has a defined and Active Process Owner / Data Steward
- *Processes can be Measured, Controlled, and Improved (6 Sigma)*

7.5.3 Business Rules

Once processes are identified and documented, business rules need to be in place for standardization and ownership.

Rules are like a guidance system:

- They provide "atomic" definitions
- Example on "Yield"
    - ✓ Must Be Numeric
    - ✓ Must be between 0 and 100 (inclusive)
    - ✓ Must be "Attached" to a Product
    - ✓ Must be Updated At least 1/year
    - ✓ If Parts > 1 yr. Old Must be >95% (or exception process handles)

Figure 7.11 shows tracking of metrics by business rules. MPA is master planning analyst.

The metrics show defects going down by business rule number 205. The rule is to match a Bill of Material to a parameter missing. The total defects by MPA are high. The metrics show the proportion of those defects relevant to a certain rule number.

Figure 7.11: Metrics to Business Rules

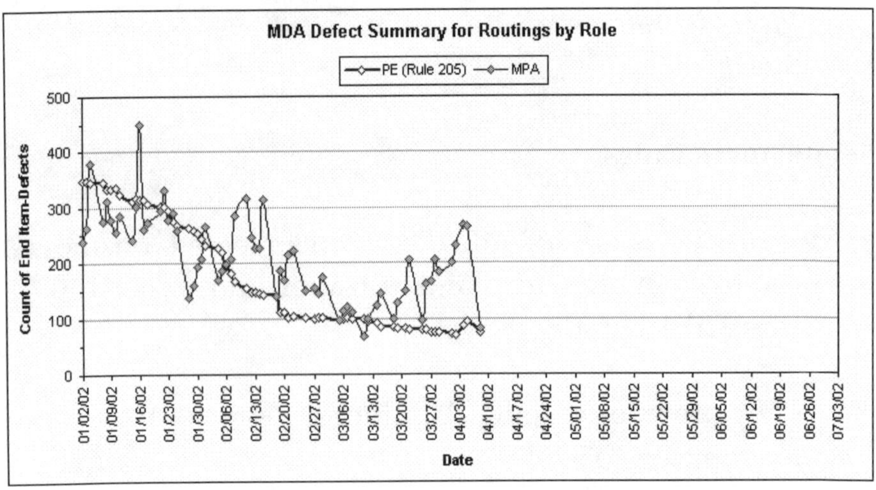

Figure 7.12 provides a sample check list for data process design. This can be a working checklist for data and business processes.

Figure 7.12: Data Process Design

Business Process Checklist ***Process Name Here***	**Data Process Checklist** ***Process Name Here***	**1**
Business Process for this request	Data element(s) for this request	
What data or information is needed to start the process?	List all systems through which this data element will flow.	
What data or information is required during the business proces?	How is the data used in each system?	
What are the outputs of the business process? Ex: Document, Decision, Positin, etc.	For each system, what are the data outputs?	
How is the data or information obtained? Is it manually entered? Is it calculated within a system?	How is the data obtained? Is it manually entered? Is it calculated within a system?	
Are there any links/ dependencies to other business processes?	How often must the data be fed to downstream systems?	
Who owns creating, maintaining, or updating the business process?	Who will own the data?	
Who is responsible for the execution of the steps in the business process?	How will the data owner create a new data element? Need a detailed description.	
How will any changes be made to the process? Need a detailed description.	How will the data owner change the data element? Need a detailed description.	

7.5.4 Role of the process champion

- The champion understands process and the enterprise measurement system, such as the Balanced Scorecard
Coaching of upper management
Value and importance of process management
Champion from the operations area to lead
- Ensures that the Operational system map is clearly defined, including white space
- Strategic direction is clear – explicit that they will manage the process
- Concepts are well understood

- Planning focuses on the end to end process – we will run the business by end to end process focused on the customer
- Mapping process is a holistic view, and is easy to understand
- Focus on cost management through performance improvement
- Establishes a forum for process team to discuss process improvement
- Level of collaboration and communication is excellent on operational level.
- Recognizes that process-based management is the key to success

The point is that by focusing on improving the data process, in this case, the timeliness of this data is improved to meet the business need. Clear goals are set, clear performance to the goal is measured and shown via the histogram. The process is now capable of meeting the "time" business requirement and the data steward has the ability to monitor the process. The same methodology is also used for the quality business requirements.

Question: How do you get high quality and timely data?

Answer: Through capable and repeatable data processes!

7.6 DATA STEWARD

In this section, we will discuss the Data Steward:

- What is a data steward?
- Objectives for a data steward
- How to help the data steward become effective

7.6.1 The Data Steward

A data steward is a person with specialized knowledge of the data used or created in a particular business area. This knowledge is used to manage the accuracy and integrity of data that is "owned" by others within the organization. The historical use of the term "steward" refers to one who has accountability for managing something that is owned by someone else. A Data Steward will ensure that data stays trustworthy, timely and seamless for specific data sets by facilitating the data processes of those data sets.

When so much effort is put in for data readiness, collapsing multiple systems of record and implementation of enterprise systems, it is a "must do" to have a Data Steward.

A corporation cannot afford to go back to the status quo of "we will fix it when it gets bad again". A Data Steward is one of the critical pieces in keeping data and processes clean.

7.6.2 The Data Steward's Objective

The following points explain the main objectives of a Data Steward. He/She takes an active leadership role in an organization with the passion for data and processes.

- Improve the value and quality of data.
- Increase organizational communication, understanding and productivity through data as a common business language.
- Articulate the value of data and minimize the cost of data.
- Improve customer satisfaction and team effectiveness.
- Ensure the availability of appropriate training for data users.
- Promote the importance of "data investment" to other organizations.
- Implement critical metric standards to allow comprehensive evaluation of the health of the data.

There are various challenges in carrying out this role. The most important one is becoming a change agent and taking an influence manager's role. Other challenges are:

- Motivation of data owners to participate in the accuracy and integrity of their data.
- Collaboration and communication between data stakeholders.
- Cultural resistance to the adherence of data processes.
- Insufficient management buy-in to data processes.

- Data owners typically have no job descriptions enforcing "data ownership" responsibilities.
- Proactively monitor data and process metrics and drive continuous improvement, by taking ownership of metric and keeping it at a sustainable level.
- Coordinate weekly or bi-weekly meetings with other analysts and subject matter experts for each area to discuss topics related to the business process, metrics, and other issues.
- Communicate technical issues to the Technical Support person.
- Maintenance and update of business rules and business processes.
- Knowledgeable of tools associated with data, processes and systems in order to make sound decisions and recommendations.
- Work with appropriate personnel to enhance and maintain tools and training documents.
- Motivate other stewards and subject matter experts in the accuracy and integrity of their data.

To carry out this role, the authors have found that a Data Steward spends as much as 50% of time dedicated to this effort. The objective is to recognize a single point of contact to management.

The Data Steward is also a knowledge champion, accountable for the work outcomes of other areas for use of data, including upholding any policies or regulations governing its use. Business information responsibility extends to the validation of the definition of data, including specification of valid values.

7.6.3 Increasing Effectiveness

Most progressive corporations have linked the Data Steward metrics to the individual performance scorecard. Workflow systems are designed which would send e-mails of defects to the stewards. If this is not fixed in a timely manner, escalation to managers is prompted by the workflow system. This alerts the manager to cause continuous improvement in data timeliness and completeness. The work flow examples are discussed in chapter 8.

A Data Steward role should grow into a knowledge worker who is the data consultant for the organization, with a focus on data, data process and information quality.

CHAPTER RECAP

The five pillars approach is a proven technique used by the authors for an enterprise wide system implementation. It has also been used for Bill of Material cleanup and collapsing multiple systems of record. The authors have also successfully linked the technical and human sides of the equation, creating process champions and data stewards. With the robustness of data elements, more data stewards are created. This becomes common as the value of data is understood.

8 CHAPTER

METHODOLOGY, CONCEPTS & APPLICATIONS

INTRODUCTION

The first part of this chapter focuses on "data mining". The intent of this section is to provide an understanding of the concept of "data mining", a description of the elements required for "data mining", and a discussion of what it is not. The second part of this chapter examines some of the tools that are available.

8.1 DATA MINING

The hype – there are numerous reports about companies that have saved millions of dollars by implementing a data mining system that "discovered" unsuspected relationships that could be "harvested" by the business to their advantage. While not all these cases are absolutely true, there is substance in the claims. It has been reported that one large banking institution saved over $60M per month by cleansing, a part of data mining, their system. If one considers the costs associated with having multiple entries in the customer database, this is understandable. A multiple entry is the existence of the same key database identifier (a person in this case) having multiple files associated with that key identifier. For example, a person could be identified by a first and last name, or a first initial and last name, or a last name and then the first name. This list of variations could continue with the various elements of the address. Each of the variations causes multiple occurrences of the total record in the database.

Consider the cost associated with the multiple entries. The easiest assignment is the cost of mailing multiple items to the same individual. While the cost of the mailer and the associated postage can be easily identified, the costs of the multiple inserts need to be added into the equation. Let's assume that the database contains 100,000 entries – a very small number for most efforts. If we assume that the database inaccuracies are 10% (most are higher) then 10,000 items in the mailing did not need to be made. If we assume that the cost of the mailing was $1.10 ($0.75 for insert, $0.15 for mailing package, and $0.20 for bulk mailing), the cost of the erroneous mailing is $11,000 for this instance. Consider the additional costs if the mailing is specifically targeted at a group and the cost of the advertisement was several dollars.

There is another "story" that floats around that a company was able to "find" significant relationship among customers' behavior. One example is that by "mining" data, a grocery store was able to increase beer sales by locating the items near baby disposal diapers. This was based on examining the habits of males between the ages of 25 and 35.

Surprising? Not really. This is only a confirmation that there are relationships that can be examined, analyzed, and acted upon.

Is this something new? Not really. Consider the layout of a grocery supermarket. Why are produce, meats, and dairy products spread out into different areas of the store? The answer is obvious. Most visitors to the store will be interested in fresh produce, meats, and/or dairy products. Spreading out the desired items encourages the visitors to cover many areas of the store and purchase additional items. An older study showed the increase in purchases at the grocery store increases by $2 for each minute spent in the store over 30 minutes.

The ability to learn from customer behavior does not require the application of computer driven data mining exercises. It does require a search for answers and an evaluation of the data. The issue with today's environment is that there is a plethora of data. If each customer activity yielded 1KB of information, one thousand customers would provide 1MB of data. Add to that the additional information of credit card purchasers and the related location identifications and the total data number increases by a factor of 10 or 100. It is no longer possible to analyze all the data without the assistance of computerized systems. Let's consider the composition of the system for data mining.

8.1.1 The Data Mining System

The author's representation of the knowledge acquisition process that includes data mining is shown in Figure 8.1. A description of the process will help one understand the flow of data in the process. The data may exist in multiple locations. These are graphically represented by the 4 different disk drive symbols.

Figure 8.1 Knowledge Acquisition Process[29]

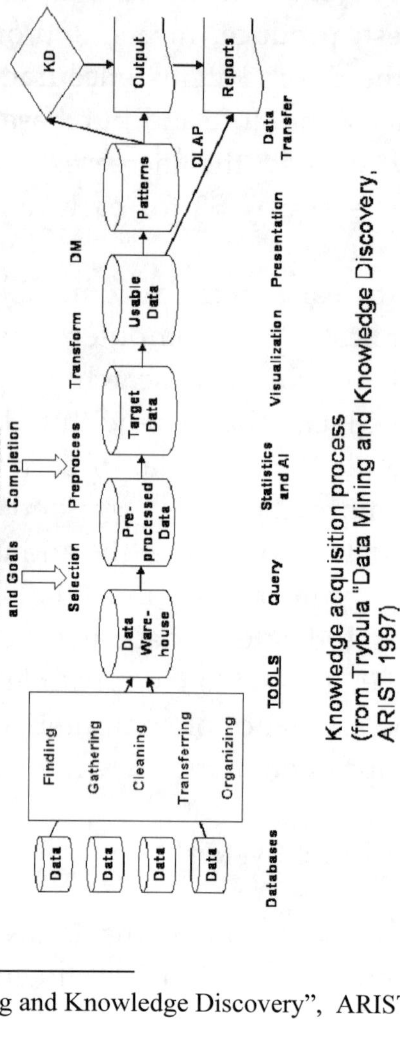

---

[29] Trybula "Data Mining and Knowledge Discovery", ARIST, 1997.

Once the location of the data is known, the acquisition process can be started. The first step is "finding" all the data. Incomplete data will provide questionable results. While this might seem to be trivial, there are may companies that have data in locations that are not normally considered for data storage. With the ability to store large amounts of equipment process data, the equipment on board storage might be overlooked as a source of information. After "finding" all the locations of data, it is necessary to "gather" it in one usable location. Once gathered, the data must be "cleansed". The cleaning needs to evaluate duplicate records, erroneous records, unwanted information, and deliver a complete and reliable database that can be evaluated. The "transferring" procedure refers to moving the data to another system where it can be analyzed.

A system that has the capabilities of drawing data from many sources and performing the previously described activities would be inefficient. The final step in the development of the data is the "organizing" of it. This could involve ensuring that all the fields for all the data are similar and compatible. If one source of data has last name flowed by first and another has first name followed by last, the differences need to resolved before any analysis in undertaken.

Having done all this, the actual process of data mining is ready to start. The prepared data is collected in a data warehouse. The task definitions and goals determine the type of rules (programs) that will be employed to evaluate the data. The data will be pre-processed to extract and prepare the data that will be evaluated. (If this is an investigation about target marketing, then zip codes and household incomes might become the critical factors. If this is about equipment performance compared with a given standard, then the equipment operational states and the inventory of the equipment will be the critical information.)

A pre-processing step analyzes the data for completeness and accuracy. This is a final check to ensure that the data has been developed into a format that is compatible with the potential analysis tools. This transforms the data into usable data. At this point, various evaluation tools can be employed for data mining. The selection of a tool will be determined by the anticipated outcome. The data mining tool provides the identification of relationships among the items. There are various methods used for evaluation, including: algorithms; associations; change and deviation determination; classifications; clustering; decision analysis; dependency; graphical; learning; neural networks; prediction; probabilistic; regression; relational learning models; search strategies; sequential patterns; statistical analysis; time sequences; and visualizations.

- **Algorithms** are the methodology employed in finding information in the database. Exhaustive searching refers to a search of all data available. This becomes time-consuming as the size of the database increases. The application of *genetic algorithms* permit a mutation in the selection process based on the concept of evolution.

- **Associations** is a method wherein the presence of one item in a data set that predicts the presence of another.
- **Change and deviation determination** is the process employed to evaluate when modifications in behavior are likely to result in other changes. (By targeting particular customers who may have reason to change banks, such as those who stop direct deposits, banks can offer additional incentives to retain customers.)
- **Classification** relates to the identification of data sets by attributes and then predicts new relationships.
- **Clustering** is a technique that aggregates the data into a finite set of categories or clusters. This aggregation or grouping provides a methodology for developing categories that can be used to represent the characteristics of the cluster.
- **Decision Analysis** can employ probability and utility theory to enhance information gathering and processing.
- **Dependency** is a method employed for looking for significant relationships between two variables.
- **Graphical** methods use a graphical structure to evaluate the data.
- **Learning** is the application of an expert system to determine the action to be conducted.
- **Neural networks** are artificial intelligence-based procedures that can learn from example and then expand that information to provide further analysis.
- **Prediction** is the methodology used to forecast results. This can be the application of probability

theory, regression analysis, or another type of statistical analysis to anticipate the outcome of the decision.

- **Probability theory** is the methodology used to analyze information in order to provide an improved outcome.
- **Regression** is a method of defining the boundary condition by evaluating the data and determining the boundary through mathematical analysis.
- **Relational learning models** are more flexible than decision-tree and rule-based approaches looking into inductive and deductive reasoning.
- **Search Strategy** is an approach for finding information in a database. Because most databases are too large for an exhaustive search, alternative strategies have been developed.
- **Identification of Sequential patterns** is a technique for predicting future activities based on observing trends. It is based on observing and recording activities over a period of time.
- **Statistical analysis** is a method employed to evaluate the structure of the database and provide for trends or missing data.
- **Time sequencing** is a method of correlating non related objects that behave similarly over time.
- **Visualization** is the process of presenting information in a graphical format.

The final step is to use the information gathered from the data. Perhaps the investigation provided information that the average age of the potential buyers of a Cadillac or Lincoln is 64 years. The question is what needs to be done with the information. One obvious answer is to authorize a survey to determine what the younger buyers are looking for and why they don't buy the existing vehicles, which their older counterparts do. Employing that data, it would be possible to add the features they are interested in to expand the size of the potential buyers. The development of an action plan based on the data is a major part of being successful with data mining.

8.1.2 Data Mining Misconceptions

Data mining is not a magic bullet that provides answers without knowing the questions. Data mining is a very powerful tool that allows one to evaluate many aspects of a business process to find relationships that can be harvested to increase the profitiablity of an organization. While there are some examples of surprising findings revealed by data mining, the questions must be worded in such a manner that the relationships are considered.

8.2 TOOLS

Within methodology and concepts, a company can develop tools to augment the Information Quality initiative. The authors will discuss two types of tools; a workflow enabled system and a Repository Tool.

8.2.1 Workflow Enabled System

For tracking metrics against data, a company needs a work flow enabled tool. This will track the quality of data and promptly inform a data owner of the health of that data element. Before such a tool is designed, a good list of business rules should be defined. In many companies, the business rules are assigned a rule number which can be a target field for picking the type of defects in the workflow enabled system. Data is then measured against the business rule. In some companies the authors found these to be tracked daily and they are also showing up on other electronic media such as pagers or PDA tools.

Another repository the tool needs is the names of data owners. A list of approvers and their manager's names are needed, if an escalation process is to be designed within the tool.

The first point of contact for the output will be the Data Stewards who have the responsibility for that data element. As discussed earlier, a good system will have the performance metrics for the Data Stewards tied to their performance plans. The idea here is that the application searches the contact for the data element, then determines who is the data steward; it then sends an e-mail notification which subsequently escalates to management if data is not fixed. The performance of the data owner or data steward can be measured by using such application.

Now the tool can collect owner responsibility at the highest level and also breakdown the data to send output to the lower levels.

Sending the owners an e-mail or notification on daily or weekly bases will trigger actions and identify data defects needing their attention. The notification is based on a pre-determined metrics. The workflow system will automatically collect the data form the legacy systems:

- By Product
- By Role, Person and Organization
- By Manager
- By Region
- By Priority
- By Time

The system must have detection logic tied to metrics and data.

The defects should be matched to business rules; in this way the notification will show which rule number is broken. By referencing the contents of the business rules to numbers, an individual will be able to develop an action plan to clean the data.

The tool can work on an ad hoc, exceptional, or continuous basis in terms of getting the reports out. The determination of these reports is made on the criticality of errors and their impact on the organization. The goal is to introduce each part into the portfolio with a complete and accurate set of data.

The escalation process, which can be addressed as "Nagware" will ensure that data is fixed in a timely and effective manner.

The mangers can roll up individual performance to metrics with a simple report writer within the tool. A further enhancement is inserting on-line instructions and web-based continuous training for the users. As far as the management role is concerned, reports can be designed to roll up individual performance metrics.

The kind of concept which captures defects and details reports can complement a company's efforts to keep data and information clean.

8.2.2 Repository Tool

The whole notion of configuration management is discussed in Chapter Nine. To make it more robust, a repository tool is required. In many companies this is a web-based tool to implement configuration management. It is a repository that can track all data-related configuration items, documents, owners, change requests, and relationships within a business process.

The storage of data and all the interdependencies for input and output can provide a good pictorial interpretation of the critical elements within the data value chain. This relationship can also point to one point of reference for critical business objects.

The advantages of this repository are that it is a growing learning tool – more data can be identified, cleaned and populated in the repository. The glossaries, business rules, tools, system of record, and data elements all in one place can provide a click-and-show type of scenario to demonstrate all connectivity of that particular instance.

Control, status accounting, audit of items and impact analysis becomes easier.

For an enterprise system implementation, this can provide a valuable insight into the architectural requirements to collapse multiple systems of records into few.

The tool can also be used by change control boards to track requests and status. The level of multidimensional can be created as this will link processes, data definitions, roles, responsibilities, systems of record, and all associated documentation.

In most companies this is linked to information system and quality standards.

8.3 DASHBOARDS

Having terabytes of clean, fresh data creates a new problem: How to turn this data into information, organize, disseminate and present it in a logical, easy to view manner?

There are a number of issues that complicate the problem:

- There are many ways to cut the data vertically, e.g., Financial, Manufacturing, and Customer views
- There are many ways to cut the data horizontally, from summary information needed by senior executives to detailed information needed by manufacturing line workers

- Every information client has a need to look at a different subset of the data
- Everyone, from Hong Kong to Poughkeepsie, wants his information on demand

Edward R. Tufte wrote in *Envisioning Information*:

> *Confusion and clutter are failures of design, not attributes of information. And so the point is to find design strategies that reveal detail and complexity – rather than to fault the data for an excess of complication. Or, worse, to fault viewers for lack of understanding.*[30]

A solution to this problem which is rapidly gaining popularity is the web-based dashboard. The dashboard of an automobile displays critical information, such as speed and fuel, in a manner that a driver can view quickly. The web-based dashboard makes it possible to display critical summary information, such as revenue and cycle time, in a manner in which a CEO or other upper level management can view quickly. Further, a web-based dashboard that is well designed will make use of hypertext links to provide drilldown functionality.

This drilldown functionality allows the user to analyze details of the summary information.

---

[30] Edward R. Tufte, "Envisioning Information" (Cheshire CT: Graphics Press, 1990),p.53

There are many commercially available dashboards that allow the client to customize the application to their needs. In general, these products come with a data repository, in which the client will insert their data, and a toolset that makes it easy for the client to implement a user interface to the data. Most provide custom metric graphics, such as meters, gauges, and dials that can be implemented in the user interface.

Another option is to design and implement a web-based dashboard in-house. This approach will take more of your own IT resources, but can be more versatile than the commercial products and with less up-front costs. One option is to use a commercial database such as Oracle for the data repository. The web user-interface can be implemented using CGI (Common Gateway Interface) written in PERL, which is freeware. PERL comes with a module that provides a means to create metrics graphics programmatically.

Whatever the solution, the concept is the same; Display critical information that can be viewed and understood quickly. Below is a very simple example that illustrates this concept and the power of drilldown functionality. We begin with some summary information at an executive level pertaining to "Widgets are Us." Red indicates underperformance to goal, green indicates that the goal has been met.

Figure 8.2: Top Level Drilldown

Overall Performance	Jan	Feb	Month-to-Date
Sales (k $$$)	12,734	11,019	4,501
Sales (k units)	3,887	3,341	1,120
Customer Complaints	53	42	11
Cycle Time (weeks)	5.2	5.3	5.5
Inventory (k units)	62,103	62,723	65,441

Clicking on the Month-to-Date number can link to a graphic such as the one below

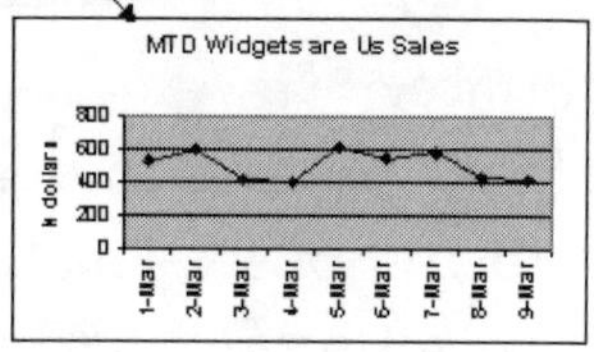

Clicking on the "Sales (k units)" label can drilldown to a regional view.

Sales by Region	Jan	Feb	Month-to-Date
US	1,987	1,812	489
Canada	826	741	202
Japan	565	523	156
Europe	509	265	273
Total	3,887	3,341	1,120

The VP of Sales might customize her view to start with the "Sales by Region" data, then drilldown to a more granular view.

Sales by US Sub-Region	Jan	Feb	Month-to-Date
Northeast	873	702	219
West Coast	644	559	158
Gulf	470	551	112
Total	1,987	1,812	489

Good dashboard design enables each user to customize his own page depending on his needs. A manager in the Sales organization might want to view the "Sales by Region" element initially, but then drilldown differently than the V.P.

One popular application from pbviews™ displays performance metrics and drilldown using a tree structure (Figure 8.4). Detailed drilldown is accomplished by right-clicking in any of the rectangular icons.

Figure 8.3: Sales Drilldown

Sales by Region	Jan	Feb	Month-to-Date
US	1,987	1,812	489
Canada	826	741	202
Japan	565	523	156
Europe	509	265	273
Total	3,887	3,341	1,120

Canadian Sales by Customer	Jan	Feb	Month-to-Date
Moose Country Widgets	215	201	57
Canadian Widgets Amalgamated	178	192	41
Widget Emporium	256	252	19
Hudson Bay Widgets	177	96	85
Total	826	741	202

Figure 8.4: Performance View in pbviews

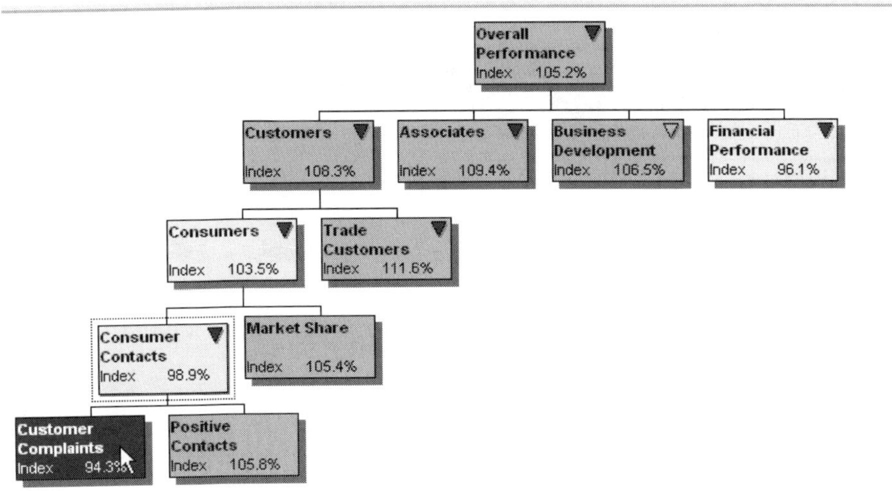

Figure 8.5: Detailed Drilldown in pbviews

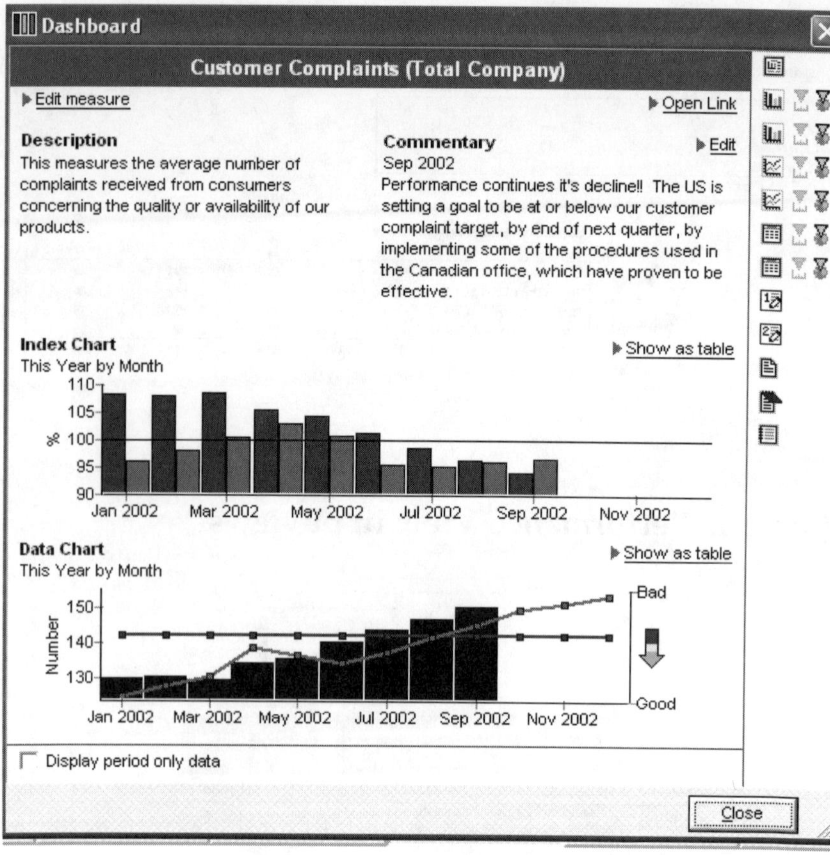

Right-clicking on the "Customer Complaints" icon brings up the screen shown in Figure 8.5.

No matter how complicated the data, customized views allow the user to look at any number of performance metrics and save them for easy retrieval at any time. The product from pbviews allows this customization using "books" (Figure 8.6).

Figure 8.6: pbviews Customized "Book"

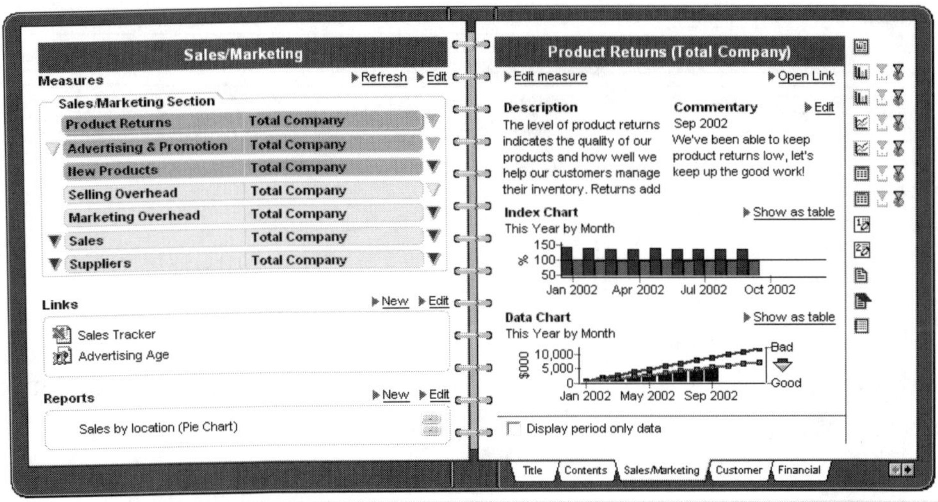

This book allows the user to list on one page any performance metrics, links, customized reports, or detailed drilldown. The tabs at the bottom of the book allows for setting up multiple customized pages. Most commercial dashboard applications provide this functionality, making it easy to design custom pages for users from the executive office to the trenches.

In Microsoft's offering, Digital Dashboard, other modules, such as Outlook, Email, and Calendar, can be added to the performance metrics to create a customized "Home Page" for the user. The website shown in Figure 8.7 was created using Microsoft's offering for their Russian sales office.

Figure 8.7: Russian Dashboard[31]

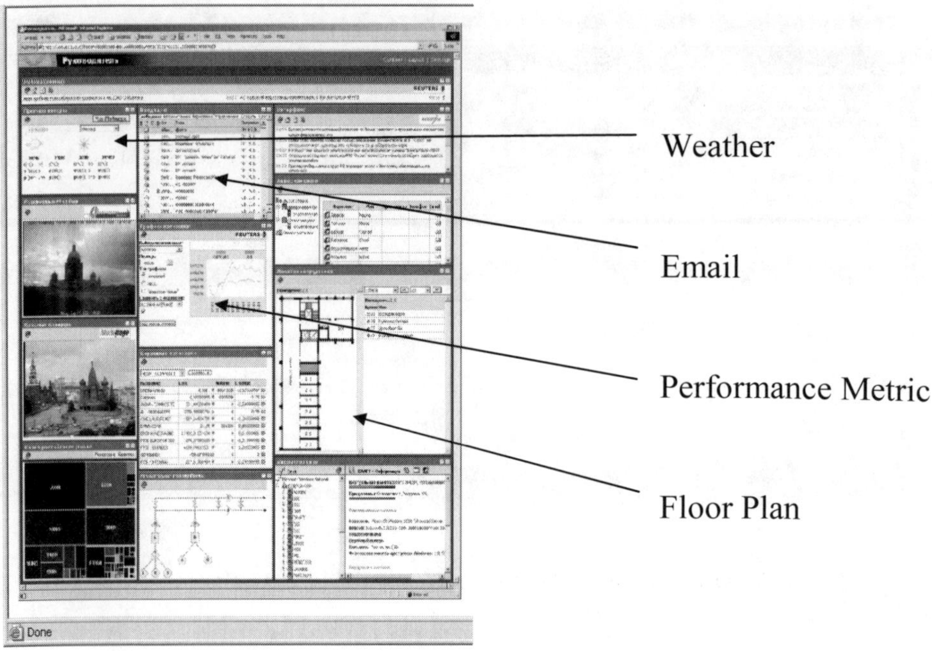

Dashboards are very effective tools in the fight against the "confusion and clutter" inherent in displaying large amounts of data to a wide variety of users. Dashboards can be designed and implemented in-house, or purchased commercially. The ability to customize a dashboard to suit any individual need makes this solution very powerful. Although rooted in performance metrics, dashboards can also offer useful functionality, such as access to email, weather and a personal calendar, thereby making it possible

[31] US-Webmasters.com, webmaster@digidashlive.com, "Russian Dashboard", http://www.digidashlive.com/russian_dd.htm

for each individual user to create their own "Home Page." For these reasons, web-based dashboards are an excellent solution when the need arises to turn terabytes of data into information, to organize, disseminate and present it in a logical, easy to view manner.

8.4 VOICE OF THE CUSTOMER

Organizations that recognize the voice of the customer as the most important aspect of doing business reap substantial, long-term rewards. Improving customer satisfaction enhances customer loyalty and improves the company's market share opportunities. However, many organizations do not understand how to listen to the customer, and more importantly, how to act once a clear expectation has been communicated.

A customer loyalty process is designed to drive actions to develop loyal customers and to increase market share with those customers. A well-executed customer loyalty process provides the following benefits:

- Documented business performance trends
- Understanding of customer expectations
- Improved relationships
- A vehicle by which to drive actions to develop loyal customers
- Improved sales account performance

This chapter will focus on a proven process for surveying customers and collecting satisfaction data, analyzing the data, preparing the data for presentation to management, implementing action plans and ultimately closing the loop with continual feedback to the customer on actionable progress.

8.4.1 Defining a Winning Team

The first step in developing a customer satisfaction process is to pull together a group of committed individuals who have an interest in the data. This team should have a dedicated sponsor, someone who has substantial influence in the organization and can motivate a team throughout the implementation of all aspects of the process. Team members should represent businesses across all sectors and regions, as well as the logistics and manufacturing organizations. Input from each of these disciplines enhances the overall effectiveness of the process and ensures buy-in when it is needed most, during the post-feedback phase where action plans are created and organizations are responsible for changing behaviors in order to meet customer needs.

8.4.2 The Survey Process

8.4.2.1 Selecting Accounts & Collecting Feedback

The process begins with the team identifying customer accounts to be surveyed for the upcoming survey cycle. Each business can select accounts based on its own criteria, which may range from key established accounts to new accounts that are strategic to growth in a new business area.

Once these accounts are identified, the sales account manager for each account is contacted to become a part of the survey process. They and their sales teams must identify the customers, by name, which they plan to survey. (See Figure 8.8, boxes 1 – 3)

Figure 8.8: Survey Process Steps

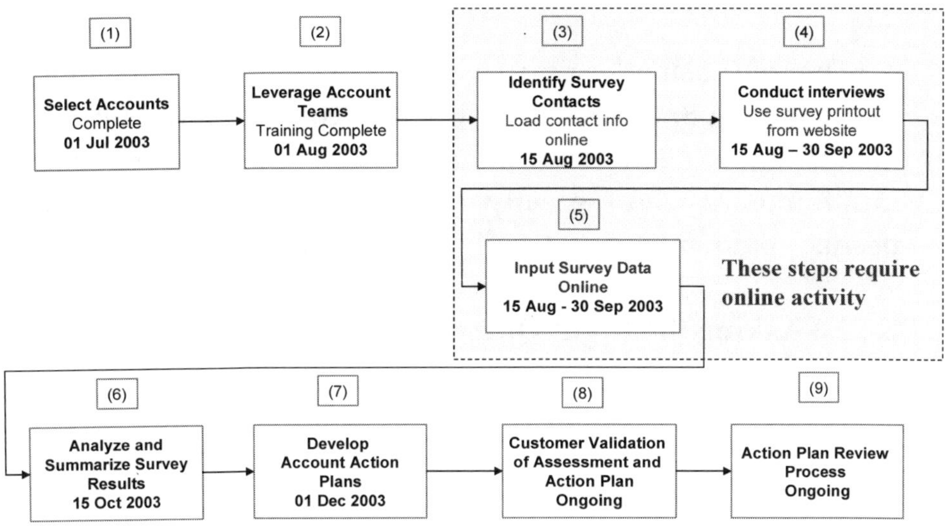

8.4.2.2 Identifying Survey Contacts

1 - Identify critical customer contacts at each account--Customers who drive vendor/product selection decisions at the account

2 – Focus on customers with functional roles such as Quality, Technology, Purchasing, and Logistics for a good sampling of inputs in all areas of business

3 - Talk to customers who are satisfied *and* dissatisfied—feedback is needed on what is done well and what can be improved. The survey's value is developing actions to improve customer perceptions

4 - Include customers who were in previous surveys and "new" customers.

5 – Include customers' not typically providing feedback through any other supplier rating process

The sales teams begin surveying the identified customers (See Figure 8. 8, boxes 4 - 5.) The best collection tool for this data is an online system. Using an online tool ensures data input integrity and greatly reduces the amount of time needed to download and analyze the data.

8.4.2.3 Asking the Right Questions

What type of feedback does the company need? What topics are important to the company? Quality? Technology? Pricing? On-time delivery? Answering these questions will enable the team to develop a set of survey questions which will return the best possible data to lay the foundation for quality feedback. Consider questions regarding the following:

- What is the customer's overall assessment of your company?
- Would the customer refer their peers to your company?

- Would the customer repurchase your company's products in the future?
- How do they assess other suppliers in relation to your company's?

Ask the customer his priority of topics from the list above, and then ask him to assess each category. Finally, and most importantly, ask the customer what can be done in each of those areas to improve and ultimately gain market share.

8.4.2.4 Analyzing and Presenting Data as Information

The survey process team can begin analyzing and interpreting the data once the surveys are complete. If the survey was conducted well, the data will produce important information to the company such as customer satisfaction, customer assessments, priorities and where the company needs to focus attention. The data is downloaded into a database where pivot charts can be created to begin the important activity of turning data into information. This information can then be used to disseminate the customer's voice throughout the organization. (See Chart, Figure 8.9)

Figure 8.9 Survey Data Example

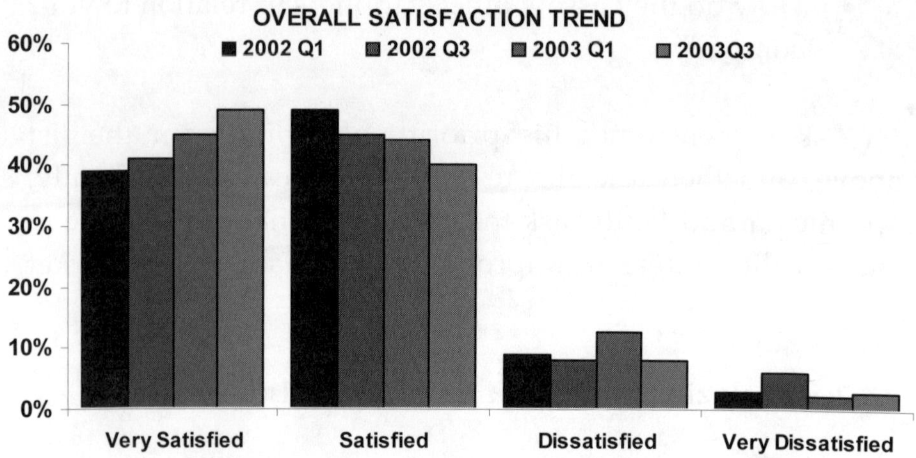

Once all of the information is available, the team should quickly (within weeks, not months) provide feedback to the sales teams who conducted the surveys, so that they can meet with their customers regarding the results. Internally, the team should meet with all levels of management across all businesses to ensure everyone in the organization knows what the customer said, and what the plans are to fix the problems.

8.4.2.5 Developing Action Plans

The organization must create action plans to address key customer issues from the survey. If this step is not a part of the performance management process, employees will not feel the urgency and ownership to address the problems. A key point is to ensure that action plans are integrated, at the highest levels of the organization, into a scorecard tracking metric. Once that has been accomplished, others will feel a much greater sense of responsibility to monitor and correct the identified problem areas. If any of these recommendations are not followed, the process will surely break down at this point. Unfortunately those organizations that do not follow through with action plan commitments are left with interesting survey data at best, and frustrated process participants (including customers) at worst.

8.4.2.6 Closing the Loop

Finally, continue communicating the progress of the action plans back to the organization and customers. Make monthly commitments to follow-through with this communication, documenting progress and areas of focus. This collaborative process enables the customer to see direct correlation between his input to the survey questions and the organization's commitment to fix the issues. Customers will want to participate in the process again, and will be eager to share their expectations during successive survey cycles. The process will translate into loyal customers and an ongoing cycle of continuous improvement.

CHAPTER RECAP

We have discussed the type of tools and analysis used in companies. As companies engage into a data readiness project or enterprise system project, many tools are designed for accountability and efficiency. The tools mentioned in this chapter are critical for such implementation. The voice of the customer, in particular, is critical to understanding gaps within the business and retention of customers by understanding the underlying data and interpreting for the goodness of the corporation.

9 CHAPTER

CONFIGURATION MANAGEMENT

INTRODUCTION

The previous chapters discussed the value of data and processes. What traditionally happens in many organizations is that there is a tremendous momentum and focus on readiness and cleaning data. The organization may have been voted world class for that effort. Now comes the difficult part: creating a configuration management environment. This is not easy, as we discussed in the previous chapters, as rules are broken.

Data Stewardship is a good notion, but to get to a level of permanency in keeping everything clean, getting business rules followed, and creating accountability, active configuration management is needed. This is by no means a permanent fix, but it creates a level of preventative maintenance and sustainability. It needs to be systemized and embedded in everything we do. More details can be obtained by referring to IEEE[32] publications.

[32] Institute of Electrical and Electronics Engineers (IEEE). http://www.ieee.org/

9.1 Definitions

The following definitions are taken from Susan Dart, SEI[33], Concepts on Configuration Management Systems:

- Identification: an identification scheme which reflects the structure of the product, and identifies components and their type, making them unique and accessible in some form
- Control: controlling the release of a product and changes to it throughout the lifecycle by having controls in place that ensure consistency by the establishment of a baseline product.
- Status accounting: recording and reporting the status of components and change requests and gathering vital statistics about components in the product.
- Audit and review: validating the completeness of a product and maintaining consistency among the components by ensuring that the product is a well-defined collection of components.
- Manufacturing: managing the construction and building of the product in an optimal manner
- Process management: ensuring the carrying out of the organization's procedures, policies and lifecycle model
- Team work: controlling the work and interactions between multiple users on a product.

[33] Carnegie Mellon Software Engineering Institute (SEI). http://www.sei.cmu.edu/

9.1.1 CMII[34] - Industry's Definition

- CM[35] is the process of managing product, facilities and processes by managing their requirements, including changes, and assuring that results conform in each case.
- The best CM process is one that can best (1) accommodate change, (2) accommodate the reuse of standards and best practices, (3) assure that all requirements remain clear, concise and valid, (4) communicate (1) and (2) and (5) promptly and precisely and (6) assure conformance to each case.
- CMII is CM plus continuous improvement in all six

9.1.2 Author's Definition

Configuration Management (CM) is the way a business documents, controls, and manages its procedures, data, and processes. The goal of the organization is to promote a culture where configuration management of all data and data processes is managed.

To recap from previous chapters, this is why we need configuration management:

- Broken or disconnected systems
- Multi-functional Database Integrity
- Limited Ownership

---

[34] Institute of Configuration Management's Configuration Management model. http://www.icmhq.com/

[35] configuration management

- Informal, Ad hoc Control Process.
- No Co-ordination or Understanding of the Total Process
- Roles are perceived as Independent, with NO System
- Hidden Costs
- Limited traceability
- Maintain Control and Accuracy of the Critical Elements of Systems Data/Documentation
- Co-ordinate the Collection of Key or Critical Data and Documentation
- Eliminate Data or Documentation Issues
- To establish Configuration Management (C.M.) as a Management Process within the supply chain
- Drive Continuous Improvement - Proactive VS Reactive

9.2 CONSIDERATIONS

As much of this requires methodology, a partnership with the Information Technology area and document central area is required. A good understanding of the operational processes is also required. Organizations need to instill an active communication vehicle which is done in a timely and proactive manner.

Continuous training is another area that needs to be targeted to configuration management. Like many change management type initiatives, top management support, endorsement, ownership and linkage to performance planning is a must. The idea here is to increase control but not place a burden on all.

Simple and standard conventions, processes and procedures should be developed. Change control boards are necessary to target customer centric requirements and maintain good quality standards. The target environment becomes a mixture of data, applications, cross-functional organizations, processes, hardware and software tools. Data, processes and systems will not be maintained and used without a structure in place. There may be good pockets of excellence in some areas, but it may be silo based.

9.3 BENEFITS

- Any changes will prompt a notification to the owner.
- A history of changes, as to who and why is captured in a database repository.
- All process changes are taken up to the change process board to promote CM.
- It is easy to identify the process, system, contact and documentation that is related to your day-to-day activities
- Provides users automated metrics on data quality through web, including email
- Instructs users on how to fix their data problems
- Distributes reports on data quality metrics to management as frequently as requested
- Determines relationship of data owner to specific data responsibility
- Core Data Elements, Glossaries and Data Definitions, Processes and Systems (Standard Data Cores) are Identified, Documented and Controlled under a

consistent Configuration Management Plan and Policy.

- Changes to any of the Standard Data Cores have to be registered and reviewed against integrity before actual changes take place.
- Key stakeholders are involved in the change reviews. Key clients are notified on the changes details, impacts, reasons, timeline, roles and responsibilities.

Breaking it down:

For a certain data element the core items can be the name, abbreviated name, definition, category, format, description, data owner, process owner, responsible organization, system of record used, appropriate documented procedure and glossary, all mapped and planned out. This should be registered in a core repository used by the business.

To drive Configuration Management, a good change control board is necessary. This should be jointly owned by Finance, Information Systems, Document central and businesses. The board will ensure that all change requests that are subject for approval gets the required focus and urgency in terms of on time delivery and customer requirements. The board will also facilitate the approval process and ensure that all stakeholders are notified and involved in the approval process. A formal registry for data elements needs to be created to keep track of any changes. Process management ensures following the organization's procedures, policies and lifecycle model. The notion of team work is propagated in controlling the work and interactions between multiple users on a product.

9.4 DOCUMENTATION

Documentation of processes, products, rules and artifacts can be an enormous task. Many progressive companies are building robust document management systems. There are multiple vaults in a company where organizations create their own repositories. Some of the areas where documents need to be standardized are:

- Global specifications
- Product documents
- Finance documents
- Sales and Marketing documents
- Customer documents
- Process documentation
- Process change notifications
- External site, outsourcing documents
- Procurement
- Knowledge repositories
- Business rules

A good approach is to get all key areas involved in launching an initiative to build a centralized database for Document Management System. Once this is done, the next target is to set up a change control board which manages the documentation in line with the configuration management policy.

Figure 9.1: Configuration Management

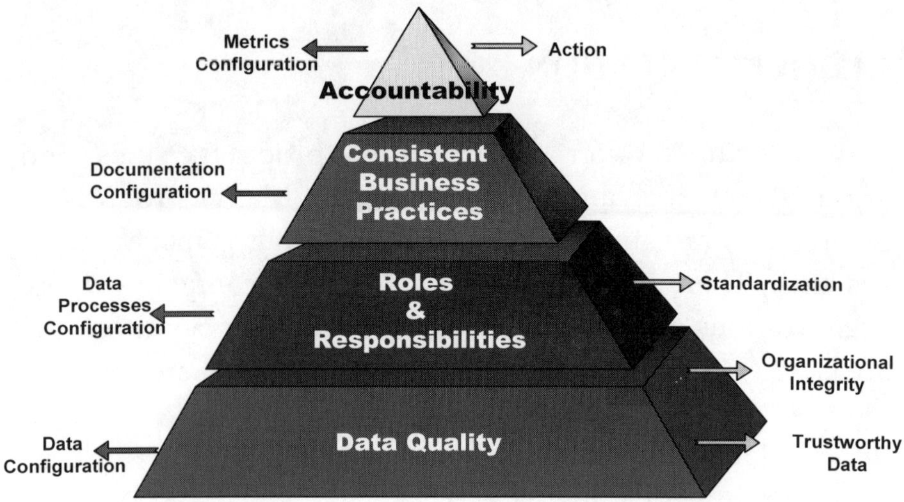

Figure 9.1 is another way of looking at the configuration management approach. The bottom part of the triangle focuses on trustworthy data. Data integrity is not questioned. Once the data becomes clean and trustworthy, the users of the processes can augment datasets in their processes. Good data processes, with clear roles and responsibilities are put in place. Data process configuration starts here. Standardization takes place with good processes and data. The documentation of this starts driving consistent business practices.

But to ensure that there is accountability; metrics need to be put in place against data and processes. With a measurement system in place, action can be taken to drive the culture of configuration management.

CHAPTER RECAP

Configuration Management drives the culture of Trustworthy, Timely and Seamless data. Some of the quick wins are:

- Identify the Standard Data Elements. Extract their definitions and create standardized glossaries.
- Establish a preventive maintenance process by starting with roles & responsibilities.
- Identify the tools for the central repository.
- Develop Process, Policy and Plan.
- Implement the Configuration Management Process.
- Manage risks.
- Create accountability and traceability.
- Create metrics, metrics, and more metrics.
- Create an early warning system.

Now to drive this, a good change management process is needed. In the next chapter, we have discussed what we have seen as change readiness.

10 CHAPTER

DRIVING CHANGE

INTRODUCTION

This entire book is about doing something different with Data Management. Given that "data is not sexy," many areas resist taking responsibility. The idea of keeping data clean and creating responsibilities and accountabilities by metrics makes it difficult to sell. An organization can build a lot of tools to configure and manage data and processes, but unless people feel that this will give the corporation a competitive advantage, it is extremely difficult to implement.

Change Management is one of the most difficult areas to tackle, particularly when the effort involves integrating many processes, functions, & roles. Furthermore, the concept of Change Management often conjures up thoughts of psychologists counseling individuals through their fear of change. On the contrary, skilled change management experts can bring a well-defined and prescriptive set of processes, methods, and practices for day-to-day management of change.

The authors have discussed ownership from the perspective of data stewardship, but the idea of institutionalizing the change throughout a corporation is not an easy task. More than ever, IT implementations fail because of the organization's lack of preparedness for change[36]. Yet, few corporations have change management areas or expertise. Change Management should be treated with the same level of importance as the technology and process decisions. Without it, executives run the risk of sponsoring a widespread change without the necessary level of assurance that the effort will be supported and understood.

Change Management is defined as the processes, tools, and techniques used to manage the people-side of a business change in order to achieve the required business outcome, and to realize that business solution effectively within the social infrastructure of the workplace[37]. With regard to data, the change management challenge is great. Data is the DNA that fuels the enterprise; however, the benefits of investing time, money, and resources to manage data are not always transparent to executives. To add to the challenge, any data effort typically cuts across numerous, decentralized functions and requires widespread collaboration and agreement among many areas. The authors encourage

---

[36] Brown, C.V. and Vessey, I. "Managing the Next Wave of Enterprise Systems: Leveraging Lessons from ERP," MIS Quarterly Executive, 2,1 (March 2003), 65-57. Markus, M.L., Axline, S., Petrie, D., and Tanis, C. "Learning from Adopters" Experiences with ERP Problems Encountered and Success Achieved," Journal of Information Technology, 15, 2, 2000, pp. 245-265

[37] 2003 Prosci Benchmarking Report, Best Practices in Change Management, p. 42.

managers to engage a change management expert with strong influence management skills up front to drive stakeholder engagement and employee preparedness.

Figure 10.1, Change Management Activities by Phase[38]

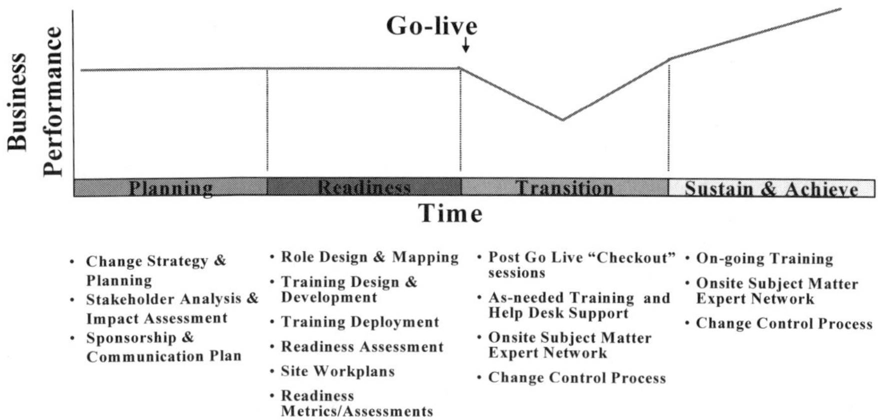

10.1 A WELL-DEFINED CHANGE MANAGEMENT APPROACH

Motorola's SPS uses a well-defined model for large-scale change efforts. For example, Change Management resources were assigned to the data team at the start of a major IT system implementation. Figure 10.1 shows the roadmap of Change Management activities that can be performed and how each activity relates to each phase of a project life cycle.

---

[38] Roberts, B., Jarvenpaa S., Baxley C. "Evolving at the Speed of Change: Mastering Change Readiness at Motorola's Semiconductor Products Sector," MIS Quarterly Executive, University of Minnesota, September 2003, pp. 58-73.

Notice that Change Management activities are performed throughout the entire project life cycle.

10.1.1 Planning Phase

The planning phase involves conducting all of the necessary stakeholder analysis and preparing a well-defined course of action for achieving buy-in and engaging key individuals at each level of the organization. This includes developing a change strategy and tactical plan, conducting a stakeholder analysis and impact assessment, and developing a sponsorship and communication plan. The change strategy and plan involves building specific change management activity and accountability into the overall project plan. A stakeholder analysis and impact assessment is then conducted to identify all existing stakeholders and subsequently determine the scope of change for each audience in terms of business processes, role, technology, or organization structure. This becomes an input into building the sponsorship and communication plan. This plan defines a robust sponsorship network of influential individuals ranging from executive level to the end-user level. The expectation of each sponsor and/or stakeholder is well communicated to avoid confusion. The plan also defines the path for communications and involvement throughout the subsequent phases and becomes the starting point for moving into the readiness phase.

10.1.2 Readiness Phase

The readiness phase is the point at which stakeholders at all levels become actively engaged. For example, a major role change called the Data Steward role is identified as part of the stakeholder analysis. Using a technique called role design and mapping, the first step is to define the parameters of that role, how the role integrates with the new process and technology, and who receives the role.

After the role is designed, the training preparation follows. This is the most important part of this phase; ensuring that each individual is equipped with the right level of knowledge and skill to perform the new role.

Readiness assessments, metrics, and site workplans are developed in parallel to the training efforts to ensure the stakeholder community's awareness and preparation are proceeding according to plan. The assessment tools are designed to measure stakeholder readiness in quantifiable terms. Regular meetings to review the assessments bring the key sponsors and leaders together at key points to monitor progress and ensure critical issues are resolved. They also provided a forum for stakeholders to escalate critical issues to a cross-functional group of leadership. As this is a continuous process, many problems can be discovered early on, allowing the sponsors and the team time to correct them prior to implementation.

10.1.3 Transition Phase

The most important objective of the transition phase is to ensure business continuity. The success of this phase is largely a measure of how activities in the previous phases were conducted. With proper planning and readiness, along with having some key additional supporting mechanisms in place, a smooth transition phase can be expected with minimal decline in business performance. Some of the key support mechanisms to have in place at this time include refresher training, post go-live checkout sessions, and an onsite network of subject matter experts to encourage on-going learning at the local levels.

10.1.4 Achievement & Sustainment Phase

The goal of the Sustain and Achieve Phase is to ensure that mechanisms are in place to foster institutionalization of the change. Prior to the project team disbanding, resources for on-going training support should be put in place. Additionally, subject matter experts in each area at the local levels should maintain their role as go-to points for new employees or to clarify information for existing employees.

Finally, an ongoing change control process, led by a cross-functional board, should be implemented to manage any future changes or modifications.

10.2 STAGES OF COMMITMENT

Another way to look at change is to consider the multiple stages an individual moves through, from unawareness to acceptance. Consider what activities to perform during each phase of the individual change curve and how much time is appropriate to allocate to each. For a visual of this concept, Figure 10.2 shows a model developed by Daryl R. Conner of Organization Development Research[39].

Figure 10.2: Stages of Commitment

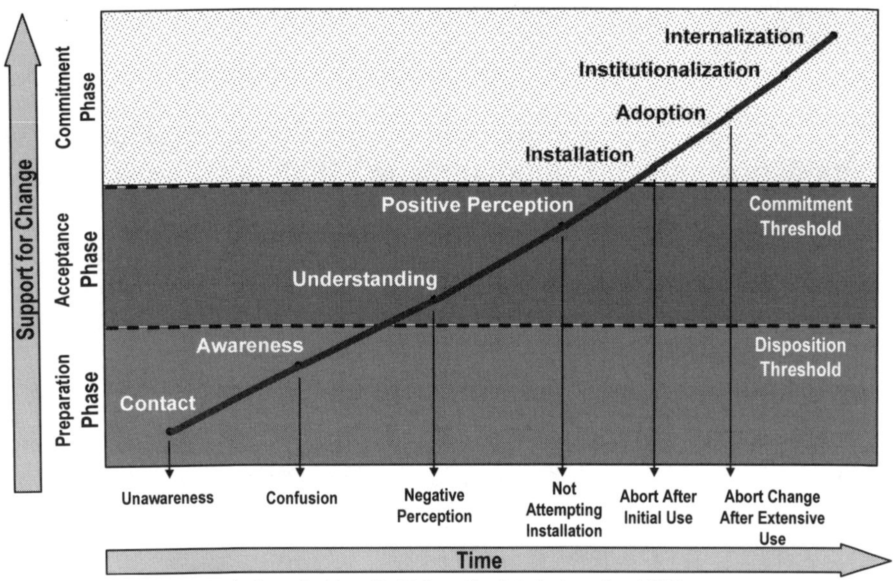

These concepts are based on the research and theory of Daryl R. Conner of Organization Development Research (ODR).
The actual change band is developed from the "Commitment Model" as outlined in Conner's book, *Managing at the Speed of Change - 1993.*

---

[39] These concepts are based on the research and theory of Daryl R. Conner of Organization Development Research (ODR). The actual change band is developed from the "Commitment Model" as outlined in Conner's book, *Managing at the Speed of Change - 1993.*

An individual's support for a change moves through three phases; preparation phase, acceptance phase, and commitment phase. The preparation phase consists of the initial contact with the stakeholders and developing awareness of why the change is happening, and how it will impact them. If readiness activities associated with moving an individual through this phase are ignored, awareness will not be achieved and only confusion will remain.

The acceptance phase is about communicating how the change relates to the individual so that understanding and a positive perception can be achieved. If this is skipped, negative perceptions can sabotage the effort and barriers to installation become significant.

The third phase is the commitment phase. This phase follows a successful installation and if all of the appropriate steps are followed, individuals will very likely move into the committed phase. They will also be more inclined to adopt what has been presented. Once the concept is adopted, institutionalization is achievable. The success stories will then begin to spread and individuals will own the change. This leads to full commitment on the part of the individual and full internalization of the change for the organization.

CHAPTER RECAP

Regardless of what model is used, a well-defined Change Management approach mitigates risk of project failure and teaches every individual at all levels of the organization to perform a specific role within the data stewardship process.

The tactics contribute significantly to building ownership over data, building accountability, and gaining collaboration at all levels of the organization. Furthermore, applying these processes systematically and repeatedly across subsequent efforts continues to contribute to achieving the desired data culture. Some key points to remember:

- Treat Change Management as an integral part of every project phase
- Dedicate resources to defining roles and delivering training
- Define an objective and quantifiable process for measuring stakeholder readiness

Finally, the success of the transition is a measure of how well change activities were conducted in the planning and readiness phase. If all the steps are followed, the change will achieve widespread acceptance. Once acceptance is reached, a strong change control process coupled with a network of subject matter experts at the local level will keep your data trustworthy, timeless, and seamless.

11 CHAPTER

STANDARDS

INTRODUCTION

With the growth of the global economy, the incorporation of data from customers, partners and suppliers is becoming a real challenge in today's enterprise. To ensure data is trustworthy, timely and seamless, the utilization of data and process standards is becoming critical. In the past few years, we have seen an explosion of global partnerships as visionary companies have developed new paradigms for doing business for the future. Such partnerships have accelerated the need for, and movement towards, data and business process standards.

Many companies are discovering whole new approaches to conducting business and even new business opportunities not previously available. Looking forward, companies will need to make use of standards to effectively compete in the global economy. Whether the goal is minimizing data errors, reduction of manual human data entry or creating new supply chain processes, the use of data and process standards plays an increasingly important role in enabling new ways of doing business. The complexities and "touch points" where business process and data standards can provide value are illustrated in Figure 11.1.

Figure 11.1: The Enterprise with Poor Data Processes & Standards

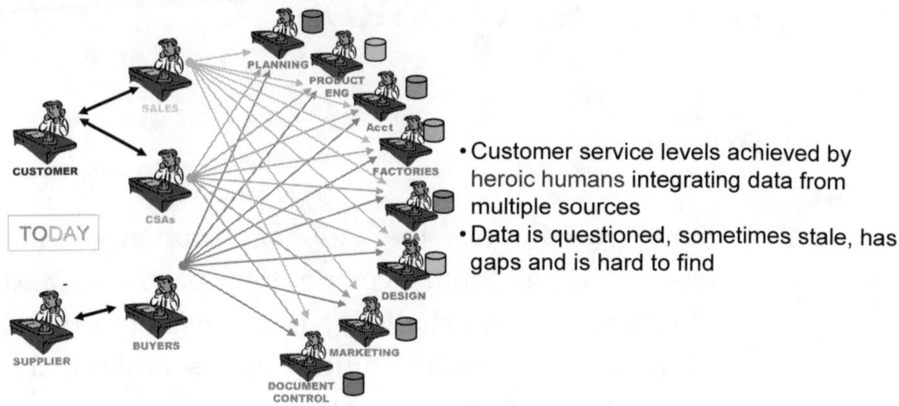

By understanding the standards efforts underway, the enterprise can incorporate their use where they provide value and begin to reap the benefits of increased flexibility and faster integration with customers, partner and suppliers.

Figure 11.2: The Enterprise with Good Data Processes & Standards

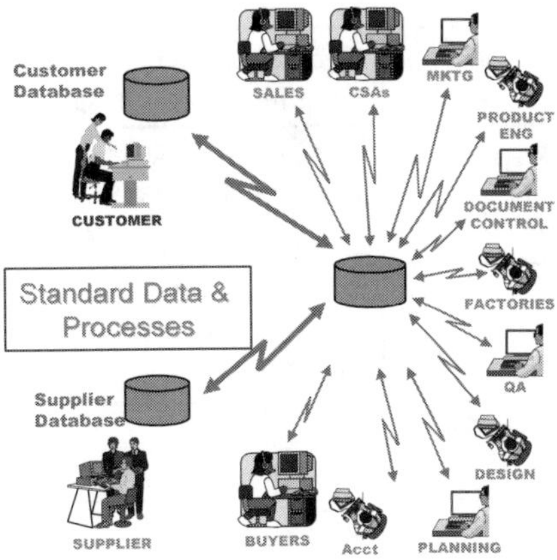

- Faster integration achieved sharing data via an emerging set of data standards
- Data is trustworthy, timely and seamless

11.1 CURRENT STANDARDS TRENDS

Standards have been in the corporate landscape for years, but with the manifestation of the Internet there has been an emergence of standards efforts for doing business via the Internet. Because the Internet is redefining how business operations, product design and development, procurement, production, inventory, distribution and sales and marketing are conducted, our focus here is on data standards efforts for data and processes via the Internet. The table below represents but a limited list of some of the more common Internet standards efforts considered interesting and/or important for today's enterprise to take into consideration.

Figure 11.3: Data Standards for the Internet

Standard	*Description*	*Related Organizations*
EDI	Electronic Data Interchange	Accredited Standards Committee (ASC) X12
XML	Extensible Markup Language	Worldwide Web Consortium (W3C), ASC X12, RosettaNet, OASIS
SOAP	Simple Object Access Protocol [SOAP}	Worldwide Web Consortium (W3C), OASIS
WSDL	Web Service Definition Language	W3C
RosettaNet	XML Standards Consortium	EDIX, W3C

11.2 EDI STANDARDS[40]

Electronic Data Interchange (EDI) is the computer-to-computer exchange of business data in standard formats. In EDI, information is organized according to a specified format set by both parties, allowing a "hands-off" computer transaction that requires no human intervention or re-keying on either end. All information contained in an EDI transaction set is, for the most part, the same as on a conventionally printed document. The EDI standards are developed and maintained by the Accredited Standards Committee (ASC) X12. The standards are designed to work across industry and company boundaries. Changes and

---

[40] Developed and maintained by the Accredited Standards Committee (ASC) X12

updates to the standards are made by consensus, reflecting the needs of the entire base of standards users, rather than those of a single organization or business sector. Today, more than 300,000 organizations use the 300+ EDI transaction sets to conduct business.

11.3 XML STANDARDS

XML, or eXtensible Markup Language, is a newer high-powered Web language developed for e-business. Unlike HTML that displays text and images now found on Web pages, XML enables the exchange of structured data over the Internet. ASC X12 is working diligently to enhance communications around the world by collaborating on the Electronic Business XML (ebXML) initiative-a worldwide effort to develop a common framework for XML business messages. The XML standards proposed by X12, are based on over twenty years of rich business semantic development. Through ASC X12 membership, your company can be an active participant and supporter of this e-business standards development process.

11.4 SOAP STANDARDS

SOAP is intended for exchanging structured information in a decentralized, distributed environment. It is an XML-based messaging framework for building distributed applications on the Web. The World Wide Web Consortium (W3C) has released SOAP, as W3C recommended, for Web applications. SOAP has provisions for internationalization, including the ability to provide multiple error messages in different languages, encodings, character sets.

11.5 SERVICE DEFINITION LANGUAGE (WSDL)

Web services definition language standard is an XML format for describing network services over the Internet. As communications protocols and message formats are standardized in the web community, it becomes increasingly possible and important to be able to describe the communications in some structured way. WSDL addresses this need by defining an XML grammar for describing network services as collections of communication endpoints capable of exchanging messages. WSDL service definitions provide documentation for distributed systems and serve as a recipe for automating the details involved in applications communication.

11.6 ROSETTANET[41]

RosettaNet is a consortium of major Information Technology, Electronic Components, Semiconductor Manufacturing, Telecommunications, and Logistics companies working to create and implement industry-wide, open e-business process standards. Although many of the XML initiatives today are complementary, the sheer number of XML standards efforts is leading to confusion among implementers and key decision makers alike. To provide a

[41] Copyright of UCC and RossettaNet consortium

clearer understanding in the industry, RosettaNet has developed a conceptual model for defining the layers of XML standards required to support B2B integration between trading partners across supply chains.

CHAPTER RECAP

All of these efforts are underway to provide today's enterprise with standards for data and business processes via the Internet. Used appropriately they can facilitate seamless data integration via timely and trustworthy standard processes. Through careful adoption and deployment the enterprise can respond with greater speed to customer demands and market opportunities.

12 CHAPTER

SUMMARY CONCLUSIONS

This book has not exaggerated the importance of data to successful business execution. In fact, as you begin to apply the principles, practices and methods, the fundamental-ness of data to your company's success will begin to set in and you will become evangelical about the importance of data. To help you with your new vocation let's review the key principles espoused in the previous chapters.

Elemental and pervasive nature of Data

We have used phrases like "Data is DNA" and "Data fuels the enterprise" to metaphorically convey the elemental and pervasive nature of data. As this understanding becomes ingrained, problems and new opportunities will instinctively be considered from the data perspective, new processes and systems will be designed to ensure the goodness of the data they act upon.

Programs and projects

The enterprise literally depends on how well data is created and managed throughout its various processes and systems. Realization of this fact will save a company from embarking on costly re-engineering efforts, adding redundant IT systems in search of greater efficiencies and IT projects will avoid data related failures. Instead, the low hanging data opportunities will be plucked where they were once ignored in lieu of planting new trees.

Five Pillars

The five pillars of data will ensure that your approach is holistic so that your data related efforts are efficient, create ongoing ownership and prevent you from having to re-address the same data sets again.

The principles in this book are not intended to be an exhaustive study of data related issues. They are just the essentials. Make sure they are in your back pack as you work with and lead others in your company to scale your own data mountains. You will be glad you have them. It is truly our pleasure to share them with you.

We wish you a most successful journey!

Appendix A

GLOSSARY OF TERMS

Activity – Work performed by people, equipment, technologies, or facilities. Activities are usually described by the "action-verb-adjective-noun" grammar convention. Activities may occur in a linked sequence and activity-to-activity assignments may exist.

Activity Analysis – The process of identifying and cataloging activities for detailed understanding and documentation of their characteristics. An activity analysis is accomplished by means of interviews, group sessions, questionnaires, observations, and reviews of physical records of work.

Activity Based Costing – A methodology that measures the cost and performance of cost objects, activities, and resources. Cost objects consume activities and activities consume resources. Resource costs are assigned to activities based on their use of those resources, and activity costs are reassigned to cost objects (outputs) based on the cost objects' proportional use of those activities. Activity-based costing incorporates causal relationships between cost objects and activities between activities and resources.

Activity Based Management – A discipline focusing on the management of activities within business processes as the route to continuously improve both the value received by customers and the profit earned in providing that value. Activity Based Management uses activity-based cost information and performance measurements to influence management action.

Algorithms – the methodology employed in finding information in the database.

Assembly - a group of subassemblies and/or parts that are put together and that constitute a major subdivision for the final product.

Associations –a method wherein the presence of one item in a data set that predicts the presence of another.

BOM - Bill of Material. The physical hierarchy of make or buy items used in developing an end item.

Classification – relates to the identification of data sets by attributes and then predicts new relationships.

Clustering –a technique that aggregates the data into a finite set of categories or clusters.

Configuration Management – the way a business documents, controls, and manages its procedures, data and processes.

Cost Driver – any situation or event that causes a change in the consumption of a resource, or influences quality or cycle time. An activity may have multiple cost drivers. Cost drivers do not necessarily need to be quantified; however, they strongly influence the selection and magnitude of activity drivers and resource drivers.

Cost of Data Readiness –the cost of making the data clean.

Data Creation – a process of combining, deriving, or manufacturing of data to meet a data readiness objective.

Data Conversion - the transformation of data to meet a data readiness objective.

Data Element - a basic unit of data for the purpose of recording and interchange.

Data Purge – the act of removing or archiving data from systems of record in order to meet a readiness objective.

Data Rationalization – usually a manual exercise because automation is dependent upon having measurable business rules.

Data Readiness – involves defining, analyzing, planning and executing to ensure that the in the enterprise's systems are correct.

Data Steward – a person with specialized knowledge of the data used or created in a particular business area.

Dependency – a method employed for looking significant relationships between two variables.

e-business - business conducted using electronic media such as the Internet, other computer networks, wireless transmissions

EDI – the computer-to-computer exchange of business data in standard formats.

ERP - a method for the effective planning and control of all resources needed to take, make, ship, and account for customer orders in a manufacturing, distribution, or service company.

IT – (Information Technology) the name of the organization that provides, processes, and distributes information to the enterprise.

Neural networks – artificial intelligence-based procedures that can learn from example and then expand that information to provide further analysis.

PDPW – potential die per Wafer is number of functional die on a wafer based on 100% yield.

Planning Parameter - a value used to describe manufacturing variables in support of customer orders: for example, when to start, how many to start, how the factory is to be loaded.

Process – a series of activities that are linked to complete a specific output. A process has a beginning, an end, and output, and at least one clearly identified input.

Process Analysis – identifying, documenting, and studying the activities that generate a process, usually for the purpose of improving the process.

ROI – Return on Investment. A financial measure of the relative return from an investment, usually expressed as a percentage of earnings produced by an asset to the amount invested in the asset.

Resources – economic elements applied or used in the performance of activities or to directly support cost objects. They include people, materials, supplies, equipment, technologies, and facilities.

Resource Driver – the best single quantitative measure of the frequency and intensity of demands placed on a resource by other resources, activities, or cost objects. It is used to assign resource costs to activities, cost objects, or to other resources.

Supply Chain - the functions inside and outside a company that enable the value chain to make products and provide services to the customer.

SOR – System of Record. The system, including the original data, application code, and data repository that control the update and maintenance of a specific set of data. The SOR also contains a definition of the system and a definitive list of what belongs and what does not belong in the system.

Test - the manufacturing stage in which the packaged die is tested.

Visualization – the process of presenting information in a graphical format.

Wafer Fab - the main manufacturing facility for processing semiconductor wafers.

Yield - the ratio of usable output from a process to its input. (E) 2) The percentage of good product produced in relation to the number of devices started.

Appendix B

SUGGESTED READINGS

Amster, B., J. Busby, and G. William. 1993. Combining Activity Based Costing and Process Mapping: A Practical Study.

Balachandran, Bala. Stragic Activity Based Accounting: New York, Prentice Hall (1994)

Balachandran, Bala, Cost Management at Saturn, A case study. Business Week Executive Briefing Services Vol 5, 1994 pp 25-28

Balachandran, Bala and Thondavadi Nandu N. What's going wrong with Activity Based Costing? Corporate Controller, September/October 1998, Warren Gorham & Lamont

Brown, C.V. and Vessey, I. Managing the Next Wave of Enterprise Systems: Leveraging Lessons from ERP "MIS Quarterly Executive (March 2003) Journal of Information Technology 2000.

Cosby, P. B. Quality is Free: The Art of Making Quality Certain, New York, Penguin Group, 1979

Harry, M., and R. Schroeder.2000. Six Sigma: The Breakthrough Management Strategy Revolutionizing the World's Top Corporations. New York, NY: Doubleday.

English, L. P. Data Quality: Meeting Customer Needs, DM Review, November 1996

English, Larry P. Improving Data Warehouse and Business Information Quality: Johh Wiley & Sons, Inc. (1999)

Jankovsky, L. & Grimme, J. (Sept 2003) How Much Does Bad Data Cost Your Company? Jounal of Corporate Accounting & Finance Vol 14 Issue 6

Kaplan, R. and D. Norton. 2001. The Strategy Focused Organization. Boston, MA: Harvard Business School Press.

Mahoney, Fracis X, Thor Carl G. The TQM Trilogy. AMACOM, NY, American Management Association

McNair and the CAM-I Cost Management Integration Team. Value Quest, Driving Profit and Performance by Integrating Strategic Management Processes, CAM-I, 2000.

Miller, John A. Implementing Activity Based Management in Daily Operations: John Wiley & Sons, Inc. (1996)

Nair, Mohan. Activity Based Information Systems, An Executive's Guide to Implementation: John Wiley & Sons, Inc. (1999)

Learning your ABC, The Hong Kong Accountant Journal, FT Law & Tax Hong Kong – Pierson Publishing. Project Management Institute. 2000. A Guide to the Project

Management Book of Knowledge. Newton, PA: Project Management Institute.

O' Conner, Daryl R. Managing at the speed of Change, 1993.

Pattyn, Dan. Web Automation and Supply Chain Workflow: one year later, Corporate Controller, May/June 1999 – Warren Gorham & Lamont

Poirier, C. Charles. Advanced Supply Chain Management, Berrett-Koehler Publishers, Inc. San Francisco, 1999.

Riggs, David A. Robbins Sharon L – The executives guide to supply chain management strategies, AMACOM, American Management Association, NY, 1997.

Roberts, B., Jarvenpaa, S. Baxley C. Evolving at the speed of change: Mastering change readiness at Motorola's semiconductor products sector "MIS Quarterly Executive, University of Minnesota, September 2003.

Trybula. "Data Mining and Knowledge Discovery" ARIST. 1997.

Tufle, Edward R. Envisioning Information, Cheshire CT: Graphics Press, 1990.

Vadgama, Ashok. Using Activity Based Management for Project Management, As Easy as ABC. ABC Technologies Newsletter, Summer 1996.

Vadgama, Ashok and Trybula, Walt. Activity Based Enterprise Analysis through Modeling, Nineteenth IEEE/CPMT Proceedings, 1996 IEMT Symposium

Vadgama, Ashok and Trybula, Walt. Employing Modeling for Activity Based Enterprise Analysis, Corporate Controller, July/August 1999, Warren Gorham & Lamont.

Wheatley, Malcolm. "ERP Training Stinks" CIO Magazine, 01 June 2000.

Zachman, J. A. A Framework for Information System Architecture – IBM, Systems Journal, Vol. 26, No. 3, 1987

Appendix C

INDEX

MANY OTHER PUBLICATIONS ARE AVAILABLE FROM THE CAM-I LIBRARY

For information about other CAM-I publications,
or to receive a copy of the most current
CAM-I Library Catalog, contact:

CAM-I Library Services
6737 Brentwood Stair Road
Suite 214
Fort Worth, Texas 76112

Telephone 817/496/4644
FAX 817/496/4974

E-mail: nancyt@cam-i.org
http://www.cam-i.org/library.html

ABC PRIMER

Authors: Gary Cokins, Alan Stratton & Jack Helbling

This document, written with a clear, informed understanding of what ABC is all about, is based on real implementation experiences. The "Three R's" now revitalizing the way business is conducted in the United States are Reengineering, Reinventing, and Redesigning processes. Traditionally, accounting systems are not designed to deliver managerial information. Activity Based information significantly boosts the value and utility of financial data for decision-makers and empowered employees. This primer addresses the lack of awareness of what ABC is and is not. It is not written as a "how to implement" cookbook, but does give a head start for action.

Price--$14.95

TARGET COSTING: THE NEXT FRONTIER IN STRATEGIC COST MANAGEMENT

Authors: The CAM-I Target Cost Core Group & Profs Shahid Ansari & Jan Bell

This book provides practical insights on how to use target costing for profit planning and cost management. The purpose is to show that target costing is a management method that allows firms to provide customers with products that they want, when they want them, at a price they can afford, and still earn adequate financial returns.

The book extends the existing knowledge base by focusing on the details of how target costing works in practice. The authors relied on state-of-the-art practices drawn from translations of papers available only in the Japanese language and the collective experience of several world class companies: Arthur Andersen LLP, The Boeing Company, Chrysler Corporation, Eastman Kodak Company and Texas Instruments.

Materials in this book are not currently available in the English language business literature. Practicing managers will find that this document contains a balance between general concepts and technical information required for their application. Examples from industry are used to illustrate important issues and current practice.

Key topics in the book include:

1. How target costing relates to business strategy and profit planning
2. A process model that links target costing with the product development cycle
3. The linkages between customer requirements and costing
4. Tools, information and measurement systems required to support target costing

Price--$44.95

THE ROAD TO EXCELLENCE: BECOMING A PROCESS-BASED COMPANY

Authors: The CAM-I Process Management Interest Group
Revised and Edited by Dennis Daly and Tom Freeman

The goal of this book is to understand the importance of process management in planning and achieving the objectives of the corporation. The authors are process strategists, implementers and practitioners from various manufacturing and service companies, consulting firms, and universities who wish to share their experiences and insights on the advantages of becoming a process-centered company and on the considerations that should be made in migrating from a functional to a process-focused organization. The book is organized into four sections:

Section 1 - Creates the strategic vision for process management; clarifies the hierarchy and the concept of core process development; provides suggestions for introducing process management within the organization and addresses organizational and behavioral issues; and defines the roles and responsibilities of process owners, controllers and performers.

Section 2 - Provides guidance on migrating from a functionally-focused to a process-focused organization using a 4-step program to assess, develop, implement and embed process management within an organization.

Section 3- Introduces the concepts of sustaining process management through analyzing current and future-state processes in relationship to customers and markets; develops activity and process metrics relating value, time, quality, flexibility and functionality to maintain customer focus; and provides guidance for using continuous process improvement in strategic, tactical and operational planning and performance.

Section 4 - Conclusions and summary. The book is intended for business publication readers with emphasis on companies of all sizes that are exploring, planning and implementing process management in their organizations. The Road To Excellence applies both to service and manufacturing firms and target readers should be CEOs, COOs, CFOs, Support Function Leaders, General Managers and Managers throughout a firm.

Price--$29.95

60 MINUTE ABC BOOK:
Activity-Based Costing For Operations Management

Author: Timothy White,
Chrysler Corporation

This short-read manual presents the ABC concept in a simplified and straightforward manner, specifically for the understanding of non-financial management, and demonstrates that the "activity management" possibilities of ABC clearly distinguish it as an Operations Management Tool. Subjects discussed include:

Traditional overhead costing methodology
Basic ABC terminology
Implementation and software considerations
Successful CAM-I member ABC implementation efforts

The manual includes an ABC tutorial diskette developed by Storage Technology Corporation that provides an in-depth description and analysis of the ABC methodology for those individuals desiring a more detailed knowledge of ABC than the 60 Minute Book provides.

Price--$19.95

CAPACITY MEASUREMENT & IMROVEMENT

Authors: CAM-I Capacity Model Interest Group

In a competitive economy, the effective use of capacity is critical. Unfortunately, there has been no universal approach to measuring the effectiveness of capacity use. The model explained in this book provides this missing tool. The model helps evaluate and change how companies use and plan capacity.

Capacity Measurement & Improvement shows how capacity measurement can be used to provide strategic information that can help managers improve the productivity of existing capacity and facilitate intelligent capital investment decisions.

The concepts of the capacity model came from work by H. L. Gantt, published in 1916, where he focused on identifying causes of variability and waste along with organizational responsibilities for capacity. This book puts these ideas into the current organizational environment.

"Capacity Measurement & Improvement" presents; 1) A unique capacity model, researched and developed by CAM-I; 2) Templates for application and implementation procedures; 3) Straightforward definitions; and 4) Key point summaries and illustrations to facilitate reader understanding

Price--$34.95

SERVICE PROCESS MEASUREMENT: BREAKING THE CODE

Authors: K. Euske, Norm Frause, T. Peck, Bruce Rosenstiel, Steve Schreck

This document provides a comprehensive and systematic approach to developing and applying activity-based performance measurements to processes that provide services - i.e., activities that usually have tangible outputs - within organizations. While there is extensive literature on analyzing operational processes within manufacturing organizations, there is little analysis available of service processes in either manufacturing or service organizations. This guidebook is intended to remedy that gap and to help seasoned process managers further enhance their organization's efficiency by extending the application of activity-based management and performance measurements to service processes.

This document is organized to lead the reader from the identification and analysis of the service process to the development of performance measures and an understanding of cost relationships, and includes case studies that illustrate using this approach for enhancing the performance of an organization's service processes.

Price--$19.95

ACTIVITY-BASED COST MANAGEMENT DESIGN FRAMEWORK: "Getting It Right The First Time"

Editors: Ronald R. Bleeker & Kenneth J. Euske

The mission of CAM-I's ABCM Design Framework is to assist first-time implementers and experienced practitioners alike with having successful Activity-Based Cost Management system deployments. It includes the comprehensive and disciplined approaches that have been "tested in the trenches" and fully validated.

The work is the culmination of four long years of cross-industry collaboration reviewing lessons learned, reasons for failure and requirements for success. The project contributors represented some 140^{+} years of collective ABCM implementation experience….arguably the most seasoned research team ever assembled in the CAM-I consortium's 32 year history. To that end the Design Framework should be considered a mandatory reference for any practitioner charged with the responsibility of implementing and maintaining an Activity-Based Costing system.

A companion web-enabled and user-friendly toolset is also available to CAM-I members to make compilation of the assessment data painless and its analysis effortless. With this wealth of information, this robust tool further insures that organizations are best positioned to avoid the typical pitfalls for first-time implementers and achieve successful and sustainable systems for ongoing decision support.

Price--$29.95